How Do You See Us?

Our Lived Realities Of Being Viewed As A Threat

AMY NICKERSON, M.A.

Amy Nickerson, M.A.

This book is dedicated to the memory of my mother Jean Marie Boudreaux Gilliam, whose lifetime spent as an educator, activist, and relentless pursuer of equality and social justice served as a model for the person I was destined to become. Thanks, Mom, for also continually telling me, "You are a writer." Your words spoken have always come to fruition.

BRC Publishing

Phoenix, Arizona

Copyright ©2019 by Amy Nickerson, M.A.

All rights reserved, including the right to reproduce this book or portions thereof in any form whatsoever. Protected under U.S. and International Law. No part of this book may be reproduced, stored in or introduced into a retrieval system, or transmitted, in any form, or by any means (electronic, mechanical, photocopying, recording, or otherwise), without prior written permission from the author.

For publishing information, please contact BRC Publishing at drbcombs@gmail.com

Cover image: Kprecia Ambers, Illustrator

ISBN: 978-1-64764-738-4

CONTENTS

	Introduction	Pg. 1
1	Some of Our Best Friends Are Cops	Pg. 7
2	So Much Unnecessary Police Misconduct	Pg. 133
3	It's Not Just The Police Who Are "Policing" Us	Pg. 28
4	So…What Do They See "When They See Us?"	Pg. 42
5	We Are Just As Scared	Pg. 61
6	The Heavy Tool	Pg. 95
7	A Sense Of Humanity, Please	Pg. 115
8	Acknowledgements	Pg. 150
9	References	Pg. 152
10	About the Author	Pg. 154

INTRODUCTION

Recently, I was encouraged by a good friend to write an essay, or possibly even a book describing and articulating all of the frightening things that have occurred to my family members involving law enforcers. Seeing that I have been a regular contributor to Facebook and other social media outlets, posting about our myriad personal encounters and, quite frankly, "near misses" with police, it just might make sense to put something together that could help others on a larger scale. I have been known to voice my concerns over what I deem to be unnecessary and excessive practices and tactics, which seem to be escalating by the minute.

So, with all of these horrible memories of troubling personal encounters with police officers, and with numerous stories etched in my mind about what has become an epidemic in our country, I had begun a first draft of an essay, beginning with a list of all of the highly stressful and unjustified encounters that continue to reside in my memory banks. I had crafted an outline and had already identified which stories I would share, in support of my thesis statement. That was until I viewed "When They See Us."

"When They See Us," a Netflix miniseries created and directed by filmmaker Ava DuVernay, tells the story of the infamous "Central Park Five" – a group of five black teenagers falsely accused and convicted of raping a white female jogger in 1989. After watching the series, my heart sank even further into the pit of my stomach, not simply because the horrific treatment of those boys was unconscionable, but also because it reminded me even more clearly of how that series of unfortunate events could have happened to my precious son, had he been in Central Park along with the rest of them, or in any park just about anywhere, for that matter.

I knew that there was a connection between that story and my family's story – and countless other

How Do You See Us?

African Americans' stories - as it relates to the criminal justice system, courts, prosecutors, detectives, police, but most importantly – many white people's attitudes and personal convictions about us. The title of the television miniseries "When They See Us" informs us of the predicament most African Americans face when "they" (white people) see "us." What became clearer after having viewed the gut-wrenching series was how Ava DuVernay brilliantly summed up the fundamental essence of my thoughts and fears about the topic of policing, and of encounters with many white people, in general. Something happens to us "when they see us." Sometimes what "they" believe "they" see is not even there, but is merely a figment of their imaginations. Still, what "they" see can set into motion the most heinous practices and events.

Thankfully, I have never had to engage with the criminal justice system at that level. However, the fear that rests within my bones that my loved ones are only one opinion or prejudgment away from similar tragedy stirs my soul. When I think about all of the encounters that we have had, albeit nothing remotely close to the horrors that the "Central Park Five" experienced, it becomes all the more urgent for me to do what I can to appeal to those in positions of power, particularly police officers, to change "how they see us."

As I reflect on the numerous instances when I have expressed my outrage on social media concerning– Trayvon Martin, Oscar Grant, Mike Brown, Tamir Rice, Freddie Gray, Walter Scott, Sandra Bland, Alton Sterling, Philando Castile, Laquan McDonald, Jordan Edwards, Stephon Clark.... Lord knows the list goes on seemingly forever.... I am still wrestling with a pain in my inner-being so extremely deep that I am not sure what can alleviate it. I see the possibility each and every time that we hear of such a senseless death that it could have easily been my son, my husband, my daughters, or even me! I place myself in the position of the victims and feel such hopelessness and despair.

Again, thinking about the saying "when they see us," I realize that something horribly wrong occurred in every one of those tragedies, based simply on how others "saw them."

Amy Nickerson, M.A.

HOW DO YOU SEE US?

ONE

SOME OF OUR BEST FRIENDS ARE COPS

This is not Black vs. Blue.

This isn't about sides – the black side or the blue side.

This is not an attack on the overall institution of law enforcement.

Nor is this a scathing rebuke of every white law enforcement officer.

This is about my perspective, my innermost feelings about how I am viewed as a black person in America, why I feel vulnerable around police officers, and how it got this way. My personal narrative has been shaped by what I have seen and experienced as it relates to issues of law enforcement. In a perfect world, police officers are a good thing. They exist, in theory, to ensure that I am protected and that every citizen, so long as they abide by the law, enjoys his or her own life and liberty. My intention each and every day, concerning police officers, is to respect them, obey them, and be thankful for their selfless, heroic duty. Some of our best friends are cops. As cliché as it sounds, my husband's Best Man at our wedding is a cop (now retired). I even have some relatives who are or have been in law enforcement, too. They have all shared the horrors of their jobs and the dangers that come with the territory. So, at my core, I understand that we need police officers in our communities. Crime exists regardless of the race of the perpetrator. We have suffered from the criminal activity of blacks and whites, alike.

For instance, not long ago, I had to call the police after packages were stolen from our front porch. After looking at our security camera footage, we were able to see that it was a white guy in a hoodie who had stolen them. I did not hesitate to call the police to summon

help regarding the crime committed. A few months after that, we had to call the cops again to report that two of our cars had been burglarized, windows smashed, and some personal belongings stolen from the trunk. This time, the footage revealed it was two black guys who had committed the crimes. We filed another police report, shared copies of the footage with the officer, and remained hopeful that they could help stop the wave of crime in our neighborhood. No question, police officers can do great work.

By the same token, we have called cops at other times, at other residences, to report crimes committed in our area, only to be made to feel uncomfortable once they arrived on the scene. There was one instance where we were somewhat vetted and questioned by a white officer as to the validity of our claims that the residence in question was actually ours. We had to show ID with an address to prove that the house was, in fact, our house! It was as if the responding officer was thinking, "Wait, THIS is who called for help? This is

YOUR house? Prove it." After we proved we were, indeed, who we said we were, the routine police work began. However, that incident left me feeling like I needed to be on guard thereafter whenever interacting with those who are supposed to be on our side. From then on, I even found myself rehearsing what to tell the police once they would arrive, desperately hoping they would not mistake Hardy or me for criminals.

I rehearsed mental scripts where I named off the NFL teams my husband had played for, not to attempt to impress anyone, but to lend credibility to our claims that the property we were standing on was, legitimately, ours. Our house. Our car. Surely an NFL player could afford to live in this neighborhood or own such an expensive car. That was the logic I needed them to use when registering disbelief and displaying signs of suspicion toward us once they saw us.

As ridiculous as it sounds, I felt it was in the interest of our survival. I wanted them to get the full

story of who we were, and how that could even be possible before any arousals of suspicion could lead to a deadly encounter. Hmmm. I always wonder if that would be the scenario if we were white. I am not sure that it would be, and I have had countless white friends maintain that no such thing has ever happened to them. Clearly, it is all in the imaginations that pop up "when they see us." I want to believe that most police are "the good guys," and I do all I can to be "a good person," but what I have learned from experience is, it is not always in your control what is believed of you.

In society, there are always legitimate reasons why a police officer must stop a vehicle, for example. For speeding. For running a red light. For expired tags. For whatever is perceived to be a violation of the law. No doubt, we need law and order in the land. Yet, what are African-Americans to do when they can trigger knee jerk reactions or suspicions based on their skin color? Why might you be stopped when you were not speeding? When you know that you know you were obeying all laws? What is it that makes some police officers believe the worst of us "when they see us?"

TWO

SO MUCH UNNECESSARY POLICE MISCONDUCT

I mention encounters with police officers on the road because so much has happened to us in our cars or because of supposed violations while driving. We often nervously joke about fears of "Driving While Black," but sadly, it is a real thing for us. Studies have shown that black people are stopped at a disproportionate number to whites. In fact, CNN recently reported that a Stanford University study of nearly 100 million traffic stops from around the country found black motorists are 20 percent more likely to be pulled over than white drivers (Willingham, 2019). The Stanford study also concluded that the data revealed an "observable racial bias in both traffic stops and subsequent decisions to conduct vehicle searches." And it doesn't matter who you are. If you are black, it is just a part of life.

I was surprised to learn that Robert Smith, the black billionaire known for being "the richest black man in the country" (and the same man who generously offered to pay off the entire 2019 Morehouse graduating class's student loans), is stopped by police "at least three to seven times a year" as he drives himself to the airport in Texas. He has recounted how the officers run his tags and check his license, and then inform him that he was speeding or changed lanes without signaling. Smith also offered that, many times, he is sent off without a ticket but, still, "you shouldn't have to be fearful of your life (and) you should be able to drive to the airport and not be stopped three to seven times a year" (Alexander, 2016).

It is hardly reassuring when someone of Smith's stature is routinely profiled and stopped. Of course, no one, regardless of socioeconomic status, deserves to be treated this way. Still, I wonder what it is that makes

Robert Smith, a black billionaire, a target? What is it they see "when they see him?" I think we all know the truth about this matter.

On the subject of police traffic stops, we have had several that come to mind, but I am still shaken by one frightening encounter, in particular. It definitely scarred us for life. In 1995, our family was driving from Tampa, Florida, up to Panama City, the panhandle area of Florida. We were headed up to spend a few days visiting some friends who had invited us to their place on the beach. At the time, our oldest daughter was three years old, and the twins were just one year old, but we decided to brave the road trip anyway. The three kids were seated in the back, each in his or her own car seat. Fortunately, we had a roomy Mercedes sedan that accommodated all of them comfortably.

We had been on the road for about three hours when we hit a noticeably rural area outside of Tallahassee. As we drove along listening to our f favorite CDs, Hardy noticed that a state trooper had put on his lights signaling for Hardy to pull over. We were being stopped! Oh, Lord! Once we pulled over, the state trooper (a middle-aged white officer) approached our car from behind and pulled out his gun! I was terrified, and I kept asking Hardy frantically, "What is this?! What did we do?!" Hardy, remaining calm, assured me that he had not been speeding, and he had no idea what the stop was for. He had also seen the gun in the trooper's hands, but he thankfully managed to keep his cool. I turned around to look at the kids in the back seat and gestured for them to be quiet, or as quiet as a mobile preschool group could be!

I watched in horror as the trooper first looked through the back window at the kids, still with his gun drawn, pointing it at the back seat! What in the world drove him to perceive a threat from US!?! He then approached Hardy's rolled-down window, and the first question, with a pronounced Southern drawl, was, "Is this your car?" Hardy responded, "Yes, officer, this is

How Do You See Us?

my car." Then the officer said, registering apparent shock at the response, "Are you SURE this is your car?" Hardy again responded with a simple, "Yes." I looked back at our oldest daughter and remember her eyes were wide open, and she had a look of fear and of confusion. The babies were holding their teething rings and car toys, babbling as babies do, but also had started to get agitated by the trooper's gruff voice. I was hoping that they would not start to cry and make the scene even more hectic. No matter that our family looked harmless and WAS harmless, the officer still kept his gun draw

He asked for Hardy's driver's license, registration, and wanted to know where we were headed. He wanted specifics, like what city, and if we knew anyone at the destination city. Hardy answered all of his questions, handed over what he asked for (after asking for permission to go in the glove box), and I remember just sitting there in utter disbelief. I was so very terrified of the drawn gun and was worried about the trooper's state of mind – why in the world was he doing this to us?! I had heard all of the stories from my folks who had traveled in the South and had encountered racism on the road, but this was beyond belief! My mother warned me, having grown up in Louisiana and Mississippi, how things could go down, but I never dreamed that we would ever be on the receiving end. Not us! Hardy was a beloved Tampa Bay Buccaneer, an All-Pro and Pro Bowler! He was a fan favorite. He had a TV show and a radio show. He did all kinds of charity work. No, this couldn't be happening to US! But I was so very wrong, and I learned that day!

It took about half an hour for the trooper to run all of his checks and, upon returning to the car, he told Hardy he had been speeding, wrote him a ticket, and left us with a terse, "Have a nice day." That was how it ended. It was unbelievable! Although I cannot prove it, I felt a vibe as if he was disappointed that all of our information was current and actually checked out. He seemed disappointed that we were not "troublemakers"

or "imposters" after all. As soon as he was finished with us and walked back to his vehicle, I was almost in tears. At that point, I didn't even want to proceed to Panama City. I had had enough!

What remains so vividly in my memory is the look of disdain on the officer's face. He clearly had not expected to see a black family in such a car, in my opinion. I really feel the Mercedes was an issue for him, as he continued to question our ownership of it throughout the encounter. Asking if Hardy was SURE it was our car, indeed! I know in my heart that we were profiled and, once he made the aggressive approach, he had no intention of showing any regard for our children in the back, or for us. To this day, our oldest daughter, Ashleigh, still remembers that terrifying moment when she witnessed a cop holding his drawn gun as if we (babies and all) were to be feared. As if we were a legitimate threat!

The trooper had no sense of concern for the children that he glared at while he grilled their father.

He had no regard for their young, innocent lives, or how a frightening experience with an armed cop could impact them forever. Ashleigh actually had nightmares afterward and feared any lengthy trips by car for quite some time. Once we got back home after the Panama City trip, I looked into reporting the officer and registering a complaint about his offensive, frightening lack of judgment in the handling of his gun, to no avail.

As if that were not bad enough, Hardy had to take another road trip from Tampa to Jacksonville three years later, in 1998. At the time, he was looking into applying for a Law School program in the offseason and needed to take the LSAT. The only test center that could accommodate his off-season training schedule was up north in Jacksonville, so he signed up to take the test there.

Luckily, a friend of ours rode with him. He was cognizant of our fears from the previous encounter, and I had expressed that I did not want Hardy driving alone through Florida. I was out in California at the time and

could not travel with him. So Hardy and our friend, Phil, left Tampa and, once they approached Palatka (a town historically known as a "sundown town" and for its KKK activity), a state trooper pulled Hardy over. He was driving another Mercedes, this one a more recent model than before. He said he had definitely not been speeding, especially knowing that he was going through such a dangerous stretch.

Once again, like before, this trooper approached the car with his gun drawn, demanding to see Hardy's license and registration! And more questions – Is this your car? How long have you had this car? Where did you purchase this car? Thankfully, Phil was carefully watching everything and remained calm. I am also thankful that Phil was not a black man (he is Italian and Cuban), and that may have saved Hardy's life.

He witnessed the questioning, the attitude, and the air of suspicion. In those days, we did not have iPhones or social media. We barely had cell phones that worked, or that could hold a strong signal in "out of range" areas. So, there was no way to record any of it, but after the encounter, Hardy made sure that the officer's badge number was written on the ticket and that he got the correct spelling of his name. He had been ticketed for speeding, and strangely, he was charged with going 16 miles over the speed limit. Neither Hardy nor Phil believed Hardy had been going that fast, but what could they do?

After Hardy and Phil returned from Jacksonville later the next day, Phil told his wife, who was also the Executive Director of our charitable foundation, what had transpired on the way to Jacksonville. She was furious and proceeded to write a letter (on Hardy Nickerson Foundation letterhead) to Florida's then-Governor Jeb Bush, complaining of the racial profiling and intimidation tactics Hardy experienced during the traffic stop. Her letter also indicated that she had CC'd other public officials, including Civil Rights Activist Jesse Jackson! While we never heard anything from Jesse Jackson, within a week, the strangest thing

happened. Two state troopers in full formal attire showed up at the Hardy Nickerson Foundation office in Tampa to deliver a letter from Jeb Bush! They had presumably driven from Tallahassee to bring the letter. In the letter, there was no admission of guilt or reference to the racial profiling or explanation as to why a gun had been drawn during the traffic stop. There were simply a few sentences detailing the State of Florida's supposed commitment to fairness and their favorable record concerning law enforcement procedures and protocols. In a nutshell, the letter implied the officer did not do anything wrong and went on to assure Hardy that Florida demands all state troopers to follow all policies.

After that, I realized that our Director's letter had clearly gotten the Governor's attention, so much so that he had troopers personally hand-deliver his response. How many times does a governor send uniformed officers, driving several hundred miles, to hand-deliver a letter? No doubt, this was most likely due to the possibility of this being a high-profile matter, given that Hardy was still playing in the NFL, and our foundation director had threatened to publicize the ordeal. Still, none of this made me feel any safer – and my impression of state troopers had taken another hit. What did the officer, from that notoriously racist county, "see" when he saw Hardy in his Mercedes Benz? What if Hardy was alone? Could it have played out like some of the horrifying footage we see today?

My heart breaks when I think about these incidents, and I see how easily negative views of police are formed, especially when you go out of your way to be law-abiding, and that still does not guarantee you any respectful treatment. This is all ridiculous! It is also our reality. I think about how quickly assumptions are made about people, which can cost them their lives, depending on the reactions that ensue. Luckily, Hardy did not argue with either of those officers or who knows how the situations could have escalated? Still, I am convinced there are serious matters of race and racial

How Do You See Us?

profiling because I know that this does not happen to many white people. In fact, the complete opposite has also occurred concerning my family. And there's one more story that I must share about police stop involving racial profiling. In 2000, we moved from Tampa to the Jacksonville area after Hardy became a free agent and signed with the Jacksonville Jaguars. We moved out to Ponte Vedra Beach, which borders the city of Jacksonville and hugs the Atlantic coastline. Given our hectic schedules and with the kids all participating in multiple sports and other after-school activities, we had hired a nanny who helped me with errands and some childcare. She was a young, white woman who would drive the kids in her car, helping me take them to their practices and games.

One day, in 2001, while running errands, all three kids were in her backseat, and she was driving along the highway. She told us that a cop pulled her over and repeatedly questioned her about the three kids in the back. He told her that he wanted to make sure that SHE was alright! Our nanny explained to the officer that she was watching the three kids, and she was on her way to take them to an afterschool activity.

According to the kids and the nanny, the officer kept looking at them and seemingly sized up the situation, perhaps in disbelief that a white woman was a nanny to three black children. My kids, who were ages ten and seven at that time, were afraid and explained how the officer kept looking at them with a puzzled look and kept asking the nanny, "Are you sure you are alright?" What in the world could he have been thinking would be wrong? And, even worse, why was his main concern the white nanny and not the black kids?!

There was no traffic violation at all. He even told her that he simply saw them pass him in the car, and he thought, "something might be wrong." Wrong? As in, what is wrong with this picture? If there was no traffic violation committed, there was no need to make the stop. He clearly formed an impression as they drove by

and then proceeded to check out what he deemed to be something out of the ordinary. "When he saw them," it appeared to be all wrong in his eyes.

THREE

IT'S NOT JUST THE POLICE WHO ARE "POLICING" US

Of course, the problems many African Americans experience are not always at the hands of police officers. Plain, ordinary folks are often guilty of unleashing their wrath on black and brown people who don't quite fit their descriptions of law-abiding citizens. The people who do this to us – neighbors, teachers, bank tellers, flight attendants, waitresses, Air BNB hosts, merchants, to name a few, can inflict incredible harm as they profile and prejudge, sensing delinquency and deviance in their midst. Just as much as rogue police officers, they are also to blame for attempting to police black and brown bodies, and creating casualties as well. The first victim who comes to mind is Trayvon Martin, who was murdered in 2012 by George Zimmerman for appearing to be "a suspicious person."

By now, we have all heard the myriad stories of African Americans being racially profiled and harassed, sometimes even killed, over the most asinine suspicions of them. These suspicions often lead to discriminatory treatment and, sometimes, severe vigilante actions. The list of things that black people have been suspected of is enormous. In reaction to these absurdities, we keep track of the things we do that seem to generate major suspicions by white people. The list includes, but is not limited to:

#DrivingWhileBlack

#ShoppingWhileBlack

#NappingWhileBlack

#HikingWhileBlack

#WalkingWhileBlack

#BarbecueingWhileBlack

#WaitingAtStarbucksWhileBlack

#AttendingChurchWhileBlack

\#MovingWhileBlack

\#FlyingWhileBlack

\#StudyingInTheLibraryWhileBlack

\#CheckingIntoAnAirBnBWhileBlack

\#PicnickingWhileBlack

\#SellingRealEstateWhileBlack

\#BankingWhileBlack

\#ChangingAFlatTireWhileBlack

\#BicyclingWhileBlack

\#GettingMailWhileBlack

\#BeingAtHomeWhileBlack

\#PickingUpLitterWhileBlack...

    The list, as ridiculous as it is, goes on and on and on. Sadly, we seem to add to it weekly. And it is indicative of major societal problems we have regarding race in this country. This is systemic. You

name it. If a black person is doing it, there have probably been some white person trying to report it, call 911 about it, prevent it, or stop it altogether with their own bare hands. These encounters often end up bad and continue to heighten tensions between the groups. Feeling like you must justify your presence in a space to whites who demand to know why you are there, question your right to be there, and who sometimes proceed to move you from there is extreme. The people who do this are not "the police," but they behave as if they are. For black people, and most people of color, these negative experiences are commonplace and familiar.

My husband was a victim of this form of "individual policing" in Pittsburgh, PA in the parking lot at Ross Park Mall where a middle-aged white man, watching Hardy get into our car (BMW), clearly felt empowered to take matters into his own hands, even though there was no reason to. "Stop! Stop! Stop right there! I need to see some ID." "Is that your car? Show me your license!" This is what the man began yelling at Hardy as he was getting into our car, trying to put the keys into the ignition. The man walked closer to the car and continued to demand that Hardy hand over some form of ID! He then began screaming, "I am going to have to make a citizen's arrest!" Repeat. A citizen's arrest! The man did not care that Hardy kept telling him that it was HIS CAR and that he had keys to prove it. Instead, he continued, in John Wayne fashion, to demand that Hardy present his driver's license and for him to surrender himself! The nerve! Luckily, Hardy (who was mostly in shock at what was transpiring) was able to keep his composure, yelled a few choice words, and got into the car quickly and sped off away from the madness.

It is really infuriating that a plain "Joe Lunchbucket" had the audacity to harass a man getting into his own car. At the time, Hardy was a player for the Pittsburgh Steelers, not that that should matter, but it was particularly disturbing to experience such blatant

racism and hostility in a city where he was a local celebrity. Yet, as we know all too well, celebrity and fame does not protect black people from harmful, inflammatory encounters. When I think about the details of this bizarre encounter, these questions swirl in my head --- what would possess an ordinary white man to even think that Hardy was stealing a car? And what gave him the courage and boldness to act as a vigilante and attempt to take matters into his own hands (even though there WAS no matter)?

This goes way beyond an attempt to be heroic. What is shameful is that the wanna-be cop, acting so recklessly, clearly had a preconceived notion about what the owner of the BMW should look like, and it most certainly shouldn't have been a black man, in his eyes. To act in this manner so quickly and decisively means that the man was "programmed" to view black and brown skin in a negative way. He felt the inalienable right to enforce the law on his own, solely based on what his imagination conjured up regarding a black man opening the door of a luxury vehicle. Once again, visions of George Zimmerman flood my mind, although this occurred two decades before the Trayvon Martin killing. What if this man had a gun? What if he convinced himself, during his attempt to take the law into his own hands (even though no law had been broken), that he felt "threatened"? And what if my husband's life was snuffed out solely because of that man's delusions of pathology?! No, I'm not overreacting! I'm not exaggerating!

The level of comfort that the man felt to enter into a state of reckless vigilantism is the same level of comfort George Zimmerman felt in chasing down Trayvon. Thankfully, my husband is alive. But we never know, from day to day, when something like this will happen again. As a matter of fact, something similar happened to my son, Hardy Jr., in Berkeley, CA.

Hardy Jr. had parked his car (Mercedes SUV) near the Cal Stadium, where he trains in the offseason. He is a graduate of UC Berkeley and was a member of the Cal football team for four years. Former players frequently return in the spring to train for their upcoming NFL seasons. Hardy said he had noticed a car that looked just like his while he was finding a parking spot, but thought nothing of it. Simply something that he noticed. Upon returning to his car after his workout, he sat down for a second to get his breath and had not yet locked the doors. The next thing he knew, a young white woman had flung open the driver's side door! He looked at her, startled, honestly thinking that she might be experiencing some form of distress and may need help.

Before he could react, she began yelling loudly, "What are you doing? Is this your car?! Wait, this is MY car!!! What are you doing in my car?!" She then took off, running down the street, still screaming.

Hardy had no clue what was going on. All he knew was some woman had just brazenly opened his door and started accusing him of taking her car. She came running back up to the driver's side where he was still seated, and he told her, "Hey, this is MY car," as he showed her the keys. She then started up again, "No, wait, that's my car!" He continued to yell, "No!" and tried to explain that this was his car, while she was still making a scene, flailing around like a disoriented chicken. Finally, she ran down the street again, then came running back up, and calmly said, "Oh, never mind, I found my car. Yours looks just like it. I parked a little way down last night but forgot where I parked." And that was it! No apology. No shame. No awareness that the stunt she had just pulled could have gotten him killed, in some instances.

Hardy Jr. called me immediately after this happened. I was living in Illinois at the time, so I was not nearby to be there for him. He recounted the story, and we discussed all of the "what ifs" there were to

imagine. He was audibly shaken and was just in disbelief at what had just occurred. What if the police were called? What if all the onlookers witnessing that woman screaming about "her" car being stolen prompted a response similar to the one in Pittsburgh? What if someone tried to apprehend Hardy Jr., in an effort to help the woman protect "her" car from a thief?!? All of the "what ifs" are just too maddening and infuriating.

With the racial climate such that it is these days, there is no guarantee that this incident could not have escalated into something extremely frightful, or even deadly. I still cannot wrap my head around the fact that someone really had the audacity to open my son's car door and then proceed to create a scene and act as if he was a criminal! It could have been "lights out" for Hardy Jr. for a number of reasons. I am thankful that he made it through the ordeal, OK, but I'm still furious that he never once got an apology.

That's the thing about white privilege and racially-motivated actions such as that one. That white woman could care less that she potentially put my son's life in harm's way as a result of her failure to double-check a license plate! As a black male seated in a Mercedes, any "good Samaritan" walking by could have been motivated to help the perceived "damsel in distress"; my son was a sitting duck in that situation. We all know that some people act first and ask questions later. And what if the cops happened to be nearby, or what if someone called them, thinking they were doing a good deed? How would they have responded to Hardy Jr., sitting in a car that the screaming woman emphatically claimed was her car?

This was an outright assertion of guilt, an outrageous claim that a black man in his own car must surely be taking a white woman's car - a car that she failed to make sure was really hers before boldly opening his door and making a scene. The frightening thing is that, in America (historically and currently),

black men can get killed when white women scream! That's the reality! It makes my blood boil that we have to endure these types of incidents. Why are we always at risk of being a suspect for no reason?! Why does it feel like "when they see us," they are rarely able to interpret anything they see in a positive way? Considering the number of false accusations and "showdowns" my family has experienced concerning our personal belongings, personal property, our whereabouts, or whatever is deemed problematic in the eyes of white people, I keep trying to figure out what we can do to protect ourselves or to prevent these incidents entirely. And then I realize the main issue is that these types of people cannot believe that we could possibly own such things, or belong in spaces that they have constructed only for themselves.

In the case of getting into nice cars, these types immediately think, "surely a crime must be taking place." The fact that we must continually try to defend ourselves and prove that we are honest and law-abiding is draining. And many still won't believe you. Our color kicks in a trigger for some folks to rise up with John Wayne-like indignation and stand their ground, or even stand YOUR ground that they think is their ground! It's all just so heavy!

One other quick point that must be made about these types of negative encounters - many times, we hear others say that the perpetrators are simply "ignorant." Somehow, ignorance alone becomes an acceptable explanation for why we see such reprehensible behavior. While I agree that there are signs of ignorance associated with these types of encounters or attacks, ignorance is still no excuse. I am reminded of a quote by author James Baldwin who declared, "Ignorance, allied with power, is the most ferocious enemy justice can have." You see, we cannot allow such behaviors to rest in the seemingly innocuous category of "ignorance," for what lies just beyond that is a likely alliance with power, which can prove to be deadly. Whites viewing black people negatively, as a

singular response, may not present a risk, but coupled with action (or power), it truly can become a major deterrent to justice, anytime, anywhere.

FOUR

SO...WHAT DO THEY SEE "WHEN THEY SEE US?"

Cutting right to the chase, there is something about black people that often triggers feelings of terror and fear in many whites. This has been going on for centuries for a number of reasons, but primarily because of how black people have been consistently portrayed, especially in the media, as being unlawful, dangerous, and threatening. Consequently, many whites have cultivated the notion that black people equate to fear. Bad things. We are thought of as deviant. Pathological. Undesirable. I have witnessed many offensive reactions to my husband and my son while walking down the street as we approached a group of white people. Heck, I even get the looks of disdain when entering into some spaces where whites do not

expect me to be, so it is not just black males who are feared, but black women, too. They often look shocked and afraid, like they are not sure we are supposed to be there and, heaven forbid, what might we do to them? Or to their property? Or to their beloved safe spaces? The imaginations can run wild and lead to unfair assumptions and prejudiced assessments of who we really are. Many times, when we are spotted in a space that they have designated as theirs alone, unnecessary actions ensue.

Hardy and I experienced one of our first "police moments" as a married couple right after we had purchased our first home. We had recently moved into the new house just outside of Pittsburgh, PA, and on that day, one of Hardy's teammates came over to see if we needed any help and to tour the property. I was inside unpacking boxes when they decided to go outside and walk around. The neighborhood was beautiful - full of lush pine trees and lots of wildlife – and it was not uncommon to see people walking around enjoying the outdoors. Yet, it had not been 10 minutes before two patrolling officers zeroed in on Hardy and his friend. After the police car pulled over, the two officers got out, and one of them asked, "What are you guys doing here?" Hardy spoke up and said, "I live here." The officer responded, "Where? What's your address?" Hardy proceeded to tell him our address – "120 Northbrook Drive. But why are you asking, officer?" To Hardy's surprise, the officer explained that a neighbor had placed a 911 call and reported that a "group of black guys" were in the neighborhood and looked "suspicious and out of place."

Then he asked to see some ID, which Hardy happened to have in his wallet, although the license did not reflect the new address – having just moved, we had not yet gone to do an address change. Luckily, the officer recognized Hardy and the teammate as members of the Pittsburgh Steelers football team and told them they were cleared to leave. He would not reveal the name of the neighbor who called 911, but when Hardy

came into the house to tell me, I was livid! I thought, "Wow! What a great housewarming gesture!"

Apparently, the neighbor who placed the call did not realize the house had been sold (although a SOLD sign was out in front) or that the new owners were black; that there would be black people occupying space nearby. I suppose they were startled at the sight of black bodies walking in the neighborhood. At any rate, the report that the police received was that there was "a group" of black men, not just one or two. That type of exaggeration concerning what they see "when they see us" occurs all of the time.

Additionally, we lived on a sprawling cul-de-sac in an upscale development where each home rested on at least one acre of land. Thus, we did not have many neighbors, and it would have had to be ones located very near to us who could even visibly spot Hardy and his teammate, as they were less than 100 yards away from our property when the police got there.

Thankfully, nothing drastic happened, and the matter was handled relatively quickly once Hardy gave the officers the information they were seeking (and the officers, luckily, were somewhat knowledgeable of the Steelers roster)!

Still, I was livid because I knew that SOMEONE seemed to feel threatened by our presence. SOMEONE looked out the window and saw black people, which triggered something. SOMEONE resorted to exaggerating the number of people outside and used language ("a group") that prompted the cops to anticipate a crowd, when, in actuality, there were only two men outside. We had to finally put that incident behind us as we wanted so desperately to enjoy the new home we had just purchased. We wanted to belong in our neighborhood. Eventually, we ended up becoming friends with a few people up the street, but always lurking in the back of my mind was the disturbing thought – who called 911 on Hardy?!

It is hurtful and even infuriating when you realize that your race or color is the trigger for such negative responses. When the little old white lady sees Hardy walking in her direction, is what she "sees" a black man who is inclined to grab her purse? A criminal? Is that why they always seem to clutch their purses when he is around? On the elevator? In the parking garage? In the Apple store?! Is that why they seem to always rush to lock their cars when they see us? Our very skin elicits extreme responses from many whites, no matter what we are doing, or not doing.

We have experienced this all too often, most recently when an older white woman saw Hardy following behind her to a security door in our condo building, and she proceeded to turn around and tell him, "This is a secure building, you must have a code." She did not believe he should be there or that he would have access to the secured space. He told her that he owned a unit there and actually did have the code to enter. The lady then looked frightened and shut the door behind her anyway, as if to lock Hardy out of a space he should not be entering. What was triggering so much fear within that woman at that moment?

Even worse, when one of those irrational fears leads to acting unreasonably, such as calling 911 (as the PA anonymous neighbor had done), or screaming for help, when there is no reason to do so, how do the responding officers "see us" at that point? What are they prepared to do immediately upon arrival? Whose story will be believed? More importantly, will you even get a chance to tell your side of the story? There are many of us who have not lived to tell our side of the story. We have too many examples of black people who have lost their lives over a "misunderstanding," mistaken identity, false accusation, or an unwarranted suspicion that led to actions that were unnecessary. I think that in many of the instances of unwarranted police (or civilian) misconduct and excessive force or violence, the common denominator is the belief that there is something frightening about the black subject.

Most perpetrators make the claims, "I feared for my life," or "He/she was acting aggressively, and I acted in self-defense."

The threat is the green light for a supposed defense. Public sentiment and the criminal justice system are usually supportive of those who must act in self-defense. It seems to be a "no brainer." Yet, the problem with this is determining if, in fact, there really was a need to act in self-defense. Many whites, including police officers, describe having a sense of fear or terror when in the presence of black people, or "certain" black people. And, heaven forbid, should they act on those fears, causing harm or even death. They always have the ability to make the claim that they BELIEVED their life was in danger. Beliefs based on feelings. How can these feelings be regulated when, many times, they are triggered because of generational conditioning and beliefs about a group of people?

"When the color of your skin is seen as a weapon, you will never be seen as unarmed."

- Del Schilling

Maybe that is why so many of these ridiculous claims of "suspicion," "fear," "terror," and "threat" arise for those of us with problematic complexions. "When they see us," negative reactions can and do ensue, many times for no good reason at all. Internal alarms seem to go off that elicit unfair, unwarranted, and sometimes deadly responses. All because of how "they see us." There is yet another story I must share illustrating this notion of skin being viewed as dangerous and how unfair profiling practices by the police can scar us for life.

I am still infuriated to this day and cannot imagine how my husband feels whenever he sees a cop car, after having experienced such a terrifying police encounter.

Back in 2008, we were living in the Charlotte, NC, area. Hardy had just left our home and was about to run some errands and then head down to our children's school, which was located in South Charlotte. We lived in an exclusive gated country club development – The Club at Longview - in the town of Waxhaw. Hardy was driving one of our Mercedes cars (and I only mention this again because I feel it is necessary to describe what the police saw and, apparently, reacted to). After turning onto Rea Road, a main thoroughfare through town, not quite a mile from our development, he noticed a police car appear in his rearview mirror. The cop sped up behind him, put his lights on, and spoke through the loudspeaker ordering him to pull over immediately. In compliance, Hardy pulled the car over to the side of the road.

The next thing he knew, he could see in the rearview mirror three more cop cars zooming in as backup! It was like they came out of nowhere. The officer who initiated the traffic stop remained right behind him, but two more cars pulled in behind his in a single line, and then yet another cop car sped up to pull in front of Hardy's car as if to block him in! Hardy was aghast when all of a sudden, the cop immediately behind him came to the side of the car with his gun drawn, while the cop in front also got out with his gun drawn. If that wasn't bad enough, another cop from one of the backup patrol cars rushed over to the passenger's side of the car with HIS gun drawn! Hardy, utterly terrified but trying to remain composed, pressed the button to roll the window down and asked, "Is there a problem, officer?"

Then, looking around at the three cops on all sides with their guns drawn, he asked further, "Did it require all of you to do this?" The main officer at Hardy's door side said, "We were in the area." The response did not address his question at all, and, at that point, Hardy began to get really worried about what it was that they thought he had done. Who did they think he was? What in the world could warrant such a response from so

many officers, SO FAST?! Then the main officer asked, "Is this your car?" Oh no! Could it be Déjà Vu?! Hardy answered, "yes," and then the officer told him to show him his driver's license and car registration. Hardy asked to retrieve the items from the center console and, ever so slowly, pulled out the documents and handed them to the officer. While that officer walked back to his car to check out Hardy's information, the other two stayed next to the passenger side door and in front of the car, respectively, with their guns still drawn!

After about five minutes, the one running the ID check came back to the car and told Hardy that he had been speeding and handed him a ticket! "You are free to go," he said, and it was not until then that the other two officers put their guns back into their holsters! There was no discussion. No recourse. Hardy did not believe he was speeding, but after all of that, he just took the ticket. After he pulled off, one car started behind him and followed him for a short while, about another mile or two. Even simply recounting the story, Hardy becomes outraged and is still in disbelief at the behavior of the police officers. It is during such a traffic stop (if that's what you call it) where one wrong move could have cost Hardy his life. This incident predates all of the iPhone footage we regularly see today of cops acting aggressively, but what was it about Hardy and his car that produced such a frightening encounter?

What else does an honest, law-abiding, hardworking black man have to do to be treated with respect and not have to fear for his life? Hardy is certain that his race had something, if not everything, to do with the traffic stop and how it unfolded – so rapidly. He maintains that he was never speeding (and in that situation, can you really argue with them?), and believes the main reason that he was treated that way was because he was a black man driving a luxury car in an affluent part of town. He believes that when it became obvious to the first officer that he was black, he

quickly radioed in for backup. It was instantaneous. But WHY did the first officer feel the need to immediately call for backup? What was it about Hardy that made the officer feel threatened enough to need backup at all? And, THREE other cop cars to assist?

"When the color of your skin is seen as a weapon, you will never be seen as unarmed."

In such an instance, Hardy has no time to prove that he is a model citizen, a famous former NFL star, a UC Berkeley-educated scholar. He has no time to plead that he is a beloved husband and father of three. That he is a good-hearted philanthropist who has given so much to untold communities across the country. None of that matters in an instant when all you appear to be is a menacing threat. It is all about optics and perception, and, unfortunately, Hardy is proof that no matter how well-groomed you are or how exquisitely dressed you are, when it is only skin color, that is the focal point, you may not stand a chance.

Not that it should matter what one wears, or what one's hairstyle looks like, or what type of car one is driving, but we hear time and time again that those are factors as to why some white people become fearful. "A hoodie pulled up, covering his face." "Long, unkempt dreadlocks." "An old beat-up car blasting rap music." We hear lots of descriptions that are supposed to conjure up fear and suspicion. Yet, Hardy fit none of those descriptions – not driving in his neighborhood in Charlotte, not walking in his neighborhood in Pennsylvania, not entering his condominium building in Illinois, not driving on the Interstate in Florida, not getting into his car at the mall.

Not once did he ever LOOK like some of THOSE people that seem scary or dangerous, as they would argue. Again, not that it should matter, but Hardy was clean-cut, sometimes wearing collared shirts, sometimes suits, driving well-maintained, impressive luxury vehicles, and living in some of the finest neighborhoods. If he had had the opportunity to speak

to the police (or the vigilantes) before guns were drawn or other outrageous tactics were employed, then they would realize that he was, as they say, "very articulate" and clearly educated - not some criminal lurking about preparing to steal or kill or destroy. And yet, the point of it all is that none of that matters when, in a split-second, a negative judgment is made about you based on your skin color. It does not matter who you are, how much money you have in the bank, how impressive your resume is, nor how extensive your education. Makes no difference. The politics of respectability cease to function for black people in the same way as for whites.

"When the color of your skin is seen as a weapon, you will never be seen as unarmed."

When faced with an imaginative mind eager to place blame or criminalize based on race or skin color, there is not much one can do to prove otherwise. Consequently, since this type of prejudging and profiling occurs at epidemic levels in our country, many times leading to unnecessary violence and even death, the onus has been placed upon the black community to plead for our lives. We share our stories and demand that something must change to honor our humanity. This is why many of us have resorted to making the declaration that "BLACK LIVES MATTER."

We also recognize that, for whatever reason, there are discrepancies between how whites are treated and how blacks are treated in any number of situations that escalate. Using Hardy's incident as an example, would a white man, doing nothing more than driving a Mercedes in his neighborhood garner such a response? Would he be pulled over and deemed a threat, leading to a call for backup? For three more cop cars to come as back up? Would guns have been drawn on him? Even if he were speeding or breaking any law at all, white people rarely garner such a response. There is less likely to be a response where officers have some sort of fear that precipitates a call in for more assistance.

There are countless stories of black people complying with police officers' orders who never live to see another day (Philando Castile immediately comes to mind.) We are often shot dead before there is even the possibility of officers arriving at a decision about whether or not a Taser should be the first choice. It never seems to get to that point. We continually see footage of black men (and women) being shoved into cop cars, onto cop cars, brutalized, Tased, shot, and sometimes killed in cold blood. Laquan McDonald, a black teenager who was walking AWAY from police officers in Chicago, was fatally shot in the back 16 times. 16 times! How was he viewed as a threat walking AWAY from the police?

Conversely, we are reminded repeatedly that many white people, even when armed and actually posing true threats, can be apprehended ALIVE! We see footage of proven killers taken into custody alive – Dylann Roof, the white supremacist who walked into a Charleston, South Carolina church's prayer service and murdered nine black people, comes to mind. We see them being treated humanely, regardless of the heinous crimes they have committed. Somehow civility is extended to this group, while we see our own treated like animals, even when they have committed no crimes. Split-second decisions are made to spare many white lives, just as easily as it seems instantaneous, split-second decisions are made to disregard our lives!

But what about OUR lives? Don't black lives deserve the same consideration and care as we see extended to white lives, time and time again? Is it possible for black lives to be valued equally to white lives? This is why many of us have been prompted to pose the question, "do our lives matter to you?" It is why the declaration had to be made finally that "Black Lives Matter." And black lives will only matter equally when, somehow, the unwarranted suspicions and fears many whites have regarding black lives cease to exist. "When they see us," will it ever become possible that they don't see a criminal? Don't see pathology? Don't see impending danger? Don't see our skin as a weapon?

FIVE

WE ARE JUST AS SCARED

As much as others seem to be fearful of black people, we are equally frightened. Many of us become afraid every time we see a cop - every time one pulls up to the side of us or follows along behind us on the road. Even if you have done nothing wrong, the fear still grips you. And then there is fear that someone white will misjudge you or accuse you, anytime, anywhere, potentially leading to unnecessary encounters with law enforcement. The fear is real. Having all of the attributes to qualify as yet another person who "fits the description" is frightening. All of the recurring images we see on television and on social media where innocent black people are profiled and then unjustly brutalized, or even killed, sustains our fear. Of course, many of us grew up being groomed by elders to be fearful of police. Generationally, we inherit the imprint from our ancestors of mistrust and fear of police. I remember growing up hearing so many horror stories from my mother, father, grandparents, aunts, and uncles about instances of unfathomable police misconduct, use of excessive force and violence. My parents grew up in the Jim Crow South and, consequently, witnessed countless acts of violence against and even murder of innocent black people.

In my home, like in so many other African American homes, cultural teachings and cautionary tales invariably included stories about THE POLICE. THE POPO. 5-0. Given the graphic details elders would share about negative encounters with law enforcement, it was difficult to avoid viewing them any other way than as a threatening presence. Young, impressionable black children have, for generations, been schooled and warned about what can transpire "when they see us."

Additionally, many black people must balance their family's truths and cautionary tales with the counter views presented in mainstream American culture – that the police are our friends and are there to protect and to serve us. US. As a child, I remember being taught about the value of police officers. We took class field trips to local precincts to learn about police officers' daily duties. Sometimes our school would have assemblies where police officers would come to speak and discuss their roles in the community and all of the reasons why we should trust them.

I even remember being a young child (probably no older than three or four) watching a favorite television show, "Mister Roger's Neighborhood." What is different about this memory is Mister Rogers' guest was a BLACK police officer – Officer Clemmons. He, too, spoke convincingly to young viewers about why the police are an important part of every community, and why "we like police officers." Indeed, young school-age children repeatedly get the message that they must respect and obey police officers. Yet, it was always contradictory, in my mind, having heard all "the stories." Most black children must face having to make a decision personally about what they believe to be true about the police. Even having had images of a black police officer on television informing me of the positive attributes of the police, it was still difficult to ascertain which story rang true for "my people." And, as I have already proven, "the stories" can be horrifying, and ultimately contribute to the internal tensions many of us have about law enforcement in general.

It reminds me of how my husband described most of his encounters with the police as a young boy growing up in Compton, CA – constant profiling, harassment, interrogation, being shoved onto the hoods of patrol cars, and unwarranted threats of arrest – as the "norm" in his world. "Just something I came to expect as normal," he claims. Those experiences are largely what shaped his views, his expectations, and his fears. While we are supposed to view the police in a

respectful, honorable manner, what we have often been told or have witnessed ourselves instead projects them as "the Boogeyman" or some sort of Grim Reaper, lurking, watching and waiting to inflict fear and pain. And, that fear can run extremely deep. Reflecting on the primary sources of fear of police officers within the black community, and then adding to that all of the negative reports and imagery that seem to flash constantly in my mind, it is no wonder that there is such a racial and cultural divide regarding whether or not the police are allies.

No matter how much I was taught in school about police officers' public servanthood and their primary role being "to protect and serve" us, I had too many opposing "flags" in my mind that served to combat all those teachings. Flags or memories about our own personal experiences of little to no protection, no service, menacing agitation, harassment, and even pain. In addition to the painful memories, there is also the fear of being misunderstood or unsupported by those sitting in what I call "the judgment seat." Countless times, I have been drawn into heated discussions with some white people who simply are unable to comprehend that there can be two completely different sets of social rules to follow when engaging with police officers. For example, many times, the disconnect concerns their views of a simple binary that does not always apply to black people – IF you don't do anything wrong, THEN you have nothing to worry about. Easy for them to say, but I always try to educate them on our reality.

The truth for many of us, as evidenced by our rapidly expanding hashtag list (Waiting for a friend While Black, Walking while getting intravenous therapy in a hospital gown While Black…), is that we do not have to be doing anything at all for something to go terribly wrong. It is not as simple as an IF/THEN formula. I cringe at the commentary that is offered about how black people can and should avoid problems with police by "just complying." As if we possess some

sort of wayward gene that predisposes us to belligerence and unlawfulness. Enough! When we consistently witness whites dismiss the injustices and atrocities that routinely take place at the hands of police officers with comments like, "why didn't he/she just do what the cop said?" or "If you just show some respect to officers, then they will show you respect," then we conclude that this is a battle we may never win. How "they see us" and frame the incidents through their lenses of police innocence fails to reassure us that we can ever be believed. Or protected. When their sense of logic dictates that anything outside of this framework should be met with suspicion or deserves blame, then we barely stand a chance to experience true justice. We rarely feel that there is "nothing to worry about."

By the same token, these arguments tend to echo their beliefs and insistence that police officers "must've had a legitimate reason to shoot, or else, why would they shoot?" A blind faith approach is often taken concerning the officer's claims. For instance, a white cop can say, "I feared for my life" (offering a reason why he or she made the decision to use the weapon) and will usually be believed. The court of public opinion often supports these explanations for why black and brown people are routinely shot and killed or suffocated to death, or violently handled. All because the officers (or, in many cases, the civilians) declare that they were facing some form of serious threat. Make no mistake about it – American culture has cultivated the notion that we pose serious threats, even when circumstances prove that such a notion is preposterous.

Besides these formulaic assumptions about guilt and innocence based upon certain behaviors, and depending on who it is either blaming or being blamed, another issue that frequently comes up as a result of "police fear" is unexplainable behavior. Most black folks will tell you that we are instructed and compelled to prepare, well beforehand, for potential future encounters with police. This is particularly true since the advent of highly publicized police killings of

unarmed black men, women, and children. This preparation is what "The Talk" is all about; black parents and elders passing along critical information to the younger generation about what they need to know to navigate our world safely.... or as safely as possible. Our friend M. Quentin Williams, former FBI agent and federal prosecutor, has even outlined all of these warnings in his book "How NOT To Get KILLED By The Police!" But there are still no guarantees.

We offer anecdotes, hypothetical scenarios, and basic do's and don'ts about which behaviors and actions should or should not occur in the presence of police. The objective is to educate and prepare BEFORE an encounter transpires in hopes of preventing harm or tragedy. Of course, we all try to rehearse various skits about what we should say and do if and when a police officer approaches us or tries to arrest us, or whatever scenario we, as black people, must anticipate. Yet, in the heat of the moment, all bets are off. Sometimes the fear and adrenaline are so great that it is impossible to think clearly or to act rationally. So, in thinking about what happens when we fear for OUR lives, it is important to consider the emotional state of those of us encountering the police. I had a long conversation with a woman I know a few years ago after several fatal shootings of unarmed black men. She was of the opinion that anyone running away or walking away from the police must be guilty of something. I responded that, while I do not advocate ever running away from police when they have instructed you to remain still, I could understand how fear and terror might possibly lead to irrational actions, and that guilt did not have to be the reason. We talked a while about the various circumstances of each case, analyzed police practices, and discussed proper protocol.

In the end, the central question still loomed - "WHY RUN!?" We may never know, but I believe that deep psychological fears can trigger responses, which seem illogical or wrong. If you are afraid, you just

might run. For lack of a better example, I think about how many times we told one of our daughters, who is extremely afraid of dogs, NOT to run from a dog if it was barking at her. We went over the drill dozens of times. Yet, in the heat of the moment, when a dog was barking and seemed to be aggressively approaching her, she took off running anyway. Of course, that triggered something in the dog to chase her, too. We understand this logic, but in an instance, when there is great fear, we often kick into "fight or flight."

I believe this is what happens sometimes when we see footage of people running away from the police. That is not to say that there are not times when a person has committed a crime and is trying to run away, hoping not to get caught by the police. Yes, that happens too. But sometimes we are so scared that irrationality takes over. I can personally attest to the effects of extreme fear creating fogged thinking and behavior that I would never have expected of myself. One time a police officer stopped me, claiming that I had made an illegal lane change. I did not realize I had done it, but the officer's presence and the swirling fears in my head paralyzed me. I couldn't even remember where my driver's license was, couldn't get my words out to tell the officer I was trying to remember where it was (even though it is ALWAYS in my purse). I couldn't even remember that my purse was behind me on the floor of the car, where I had placed it. Complete anxiety took over me and I was rendered unable to go through any of my pre-rehearsed lines.

Granted, I did not resort to anything dangerous or completely absurd, but I was clearly not myself and did not seem to have the ability to recall any practical steps or plan that I had practiced so many times before. That is how I know it is possible for such behavior – like walking or running away from a cop when it makes no sense- to take place. Panic sets in. All logic goes out the window. Then, all you know is that you feel threatened yourself. Many times, I feel like those threats that we sense can be likened to the color-coded

threat level alert system that is utilized by U.S. Homeland Security. This system, which was introduced following the 9/11 attacks, ranks potential threats by color: GREEN (low risk), BLUE (guarded - general risk), YELLOW (elevated – significant risk), ORANGE (high risk), and RED (severe risk.) This is the most effective way that I have found to describe how so many of us feel or perceive threats created by police misconduct or harassment by civilians who seek to police us. I would argue that there are some black people who probably stay at ORANGE all of the time. I also would rate my level as falling somewhere between BLUE or YELLOW most days, simply due to the constant awareness that I must maintain, at all times, navigating the spaces where I am not always made to feel welcome.

The only time I truly feel like I am at a GREEN level is in the comfort of my own home with my family – inside my home, but once I step outside my home, it can elevate. Depends on who might be around, who might be walking a dog, and not be familiar with me and trigger me by asking something ridiculous such as, "Can I help you with something?" (I don't mean to give the impression that all of my neighbors have racist tendencies – I have some wonderful neighbors of all races whom I consider friends, and most really do "get it" concerning the racial and social injustices many of us endure.) So, not every neighbor puts me on edge, but there always seems to be one or two who give off vibes that they are not comfortable with our presence.

Another reflex that I seem to have developed occurs whenever a police car approaches me. Even though I have not done anything wrong, but thanks to our prior frightening encounters, I sometimes elevate to the ORANGE level of perceived personal threat. It is almost like a form of PTSD involving police cars, police sirens, police with guns visible. And after something particularly disturbing or violent is the visual, such as watching televised footage of an unarmed black teen getting shot 16 times, or watching

the unrest in Ferguson, or watching Eric Garner continually scream "I can't breathe" to no avail, or any number of other tragic incidents, I undeniably kick into the RED zone! In the RED zone, I am easily triggered and on guard, because whatever it is that has created extreme fear within the community has also made me feel that I am severely at risk, too. All of these types of encounters and experiences create high levels of fear. And when people walk around on a daily basis, simmering like a pot of stew, eruptions can and do occur.

What is evident is the erosion of trust that has occurred, partly due to negative personal encounters, and then partly due to what continues to happen to other black people across the country. We tell one another within the community to "be careful out there" and "keep your head on a swivel," understanding that there has been yet another display of aggression and brutality and that we could become victims, too. We are often afraid of what could happen, what might transpire "when they see us." We understand that just about any outrageous thing could possibly happen in one of those encounters. And the scary thing is, just about anything – ANYTHING - can bring about an encounter. Sometimes, there is a lull in activity, and we begin to believe that it is safe again, so we may lower our color levels – maybe to YELLOW, maybe even BLUE. And then, something happens AGAIN!

Tweets and Instagram posts flood your phone. Oh no! "Did you hear about the young man killed in his grandmother's backyard?" Oh no! With social media alerts providing play-by-play accounts of the latest tragedy, just like that, my level goes back up to RED! May Day! May Day! That is what it feels like, over and over. Complete disbelief that ANOTHER killing has occurred! Cortisol levels rise through the roof!

No one wants to be on a proverbial roller-coaster of emotions, but when you witness an epidemic sweeping the nation that does not appear to be improving, then

the heightened sensitivity to police brutality, racial tensions, and conflicts of every kind exacerbates feelings of fear, agitation, and even panic. When my husband told me that he was going to have to drive through Indiana as part of his coaching duties to search for potential college football recruits, a sense of panic set in, and my alert level rose to ORANGE. I was aware of all of the dangers lurking in Indiana – home to many KKK members and stories of plenty of racist acts.

We had a few friends and business acquaintances in Indiana, and they are great people, but the overall impression of Indiana, in general, was not good. "Oh no! Can't you get a different assignment? Don't they understand that it is not safe for black folks to be driving around in the middle of Indiana?" is what I remember telling Hardy. So, what did I do? I contacted a black friend of mine, a Notre Dame alum, who was still living in Indiana and quite familiar with its racial challenges. Unfortunately, what she told me did not eliminate any fears. She proceeded to school me up on lots of facts, starting with the news that Indiana was one of the lone five states in the U.S. that, at the time, had refused to pass a hate crimes law. Not good. She also sent me a link to a map resource generated by the Southern Poverty Law Center (SPLC), an organization that specializes in civil rights advocacy and the documentation of hate crimes. Not good. The SPLC map tracked over 20 hate groups in Indiana – including "the American White Knights of the Ku Klux Klan," "Identity Europa" (a White Nationalist group), "Firm 22" (a Racist Skinhead group), and too many others to name!

Besides the threat of these known white supremacist groups dotted throughout Indiana, I also was concerned about state troopers and local police officers who may have subscribed to similar beliefs. Historically, white supremacists are known to have infiltrated local and state law enforcement agencies throughout the country; the FBI even detailed this threat over ten years ago (Downs, 2016). That is why the fear

How Do You See Us?

is so great about the police officer you may potentially encounter – because you simply never know who they really are or "how they may see you." For all we know, the officers who pulled guns on Hardy during his various traffic stops could have been white supremacists. We will never really know, but it could possibly account for the extreme aggression towards a black man.

On top of all of this frightening intel my friend shared with me, she also advised about the specific areas in Indiana known to be historically "sundown towns," and that Hardy would be best leaving those towns alone. To think that, in 2017, I was behaving as someone from the 1940s or 50s or 60s! I was frantically putting together my own simplified version of the "Green Book," guidelines for my husband to follow when on the road recruiting! Isn't that a shame?! Could this really be happening in America? Sadly, yes. Visions of Hardy driving on remote one-lane highways in the middle of Indiana raced through my head. I had already experienced other scares when Hardy had been on the road as a college coach recruiting in questionable areas of Texas, and also in the deep South while scouting potential draft picks as an NFL coach. Staying on the phone with him late at night while he drove through rural Mississippi or Alabama on his way to see college players who lived in those places. My fears are not unwarranted or unjustified. I am not just some neurotic, anxious wife with nothing else to do! My fears are steeped in "the stories," the extensive catalogue of stories handed down to me from my family and friends.

They are steeped in the knowledge of what has happened to many black people in those areas. And they are steeped in my cognizance of how something as simple as a traffic stop on one of those roads or highways could spell serious trouble. I don't mean to give the impression that these places I mention are the only places where I am uncertain of our safety.

Of course, we can see that racism has no boundaries and can happen anywhere, anytime. Yet, if given a choice, I prefer to increase our chances of safety and survival and take the path of least resistance. In my mind, that involves avoiding or limiting your time in the places where you already know trouble has occurred or where a concentration of racists might frequent. But when you have a job to do, you can't always avoid places where you are expected to travel to, and so Hardy could not avoid going where he was assigned to recruit high school football players.

Still, the level of fear surrounding his travels gripped me, and, referring again to my color-coded threat indicator, I stayed in a state of ORANGE whenever he had to embark on such a journey. When I couldn't reach him by phone for hours, horrible thoughts raced through my mind, fearing the worst. RED again! You see, the logic or rationale stating that "if you don't do anything wrong, you have nothing to worry about" does not apply to Hardy driving around racist towns in Indiana or Illinois, or Texas, or Alabama, or North Carolina, or Florida, or California, or wherever!

All of these issues have weighed extremely heavily on my heart, so imagine my mental state and sense of panic when my son was pulled over by a cop, just last year, while I was talking to him on the phone! The crazy thing is, we had just been discussing recent cases of police brutality, and also where we both thought might be unsafe areas to travel in the Ohio and Kentucky area. It was Sunday morning around 10AM, and I had gone on my daily walk through our neighborhood. Hardy Jr., who happens to also be a professional football player for the Cincinnati Bengals, was off that day as training camp had just ended. He was on his way driving to a Cryotherapy treatment session (pro athletes often utilize this form of therapy to help their bodies recover from wear and tear) when he called me, as he usually did every day.

While I walked, we talked about lots of things – the weather, how training camp was going, how Hardy Sr.'s camp was going, when I was planning to make tacos, unpacking luggage in his apartment, when I might head out for a home game - just a normal mother/son chat. And as many black mothers do, I had the habit of reminding him to watch speed limits, watch other drivers, stay out of areas that looked shady, and to be aware of his surroundings since he was still relatively new to the area. I was just blabbing my mouth when, all of a sudden, Hardy Jr. says, "I'm getting pulled over." I stopped in my tracks and couldn't believe what he just said! He told me he saw the lights flash in his rear-view mirror and then heard the officer say, "Pull over!" He pulled over to the side of the road. Oh, no! Deja vu, I thought! My threat level began to rise! Hardy Jr. had already told me he was driving through an affluent, established residential neighborhood with big, stately, 19th, and early 20th century homes. Kind of like the "old money" sections of town every major city has. That just happened to be the route he had to take to reach the Cryotherapy clinic. I remember it specifically, because we had been discussing the geographical layout of Cincinnati and how certain neighborhoods seemed to suddenly change from affluent to poor. He had noticed that, unlike some other places we have lived, there was a different type of transition from one type of neighborhood to the next. Just basic observations we chatted about. So, I had an idea of what type of area he was being stopped in. I told him to keep me on the line before the cop got out of his car. I was worried about the imminent encounter and just started having all kinds of thoughts race through my head. I began to pray – "Lord, please protect little Hardy out there by himself. Lord, protect him and keep him safe. Amen." I then told him, "get your Pullover Pal ready to give to the officer!"

The Pullover Pal was something I had bought for every member of our family after seeing it advertised on either Facebook or Twitter. It is a document holder, sort of like a mini notebook, with various pockets to

hold all of your car-related information. It is intended to give the driver immediate access to important documents while driving and to minimize risks associated with moving to search for items in the glove compartment.

Actually, the inventor of the Pullover Pal, a black man, had come up with the idea in 2016 following a rash of police-related incidents. At any rate, I had put the Pullover Pal in Hardy Jr.'s car before he had it shipped out from California to Cincinnati months earlier. All of the current car registration and insurance information was inside it. Knowing that the officer would want to see ID and documents, I wanted Hardy Jr. to get that ready to hand over to avoid any hassles (or perceived sudden moves) trying to reach for it later. He told me he had the Pullover Pal ready, and I reiterated, "Keep me on the phone. I need to hear what's happening. And remember. It's 'Yes, officer. No officer.' Stay calm and be respectful." He told me, "OK, but you be quiet. I don't need you talking." Our phone call was connected through his car's blue tooth system so I could hear everything, and anything I said could be heard through the car's speakers. Then that's when I heard the cop approach the car. Hardy Jr. had already rolled down the window, as he had been routinely taught to do. The cop immediately said, "I need to see your license and registration. Is this your car?" Hardy Jr. said, "Yes, officer. And here is everything you've asked for," as he handed the opened Pullover Pal to the officer.

Then, the officer asked, "This car belongs to YOU? You are the owner?"

"Yes, officer."

"Are you from California?"

The police officer was obviously referring to Hardy's driver's license and

the car's California license plate (And, yes, this was the

SAME car that the young white woman had accused him of stealing back in Berkeley! Lucky car!)

"Yes, officer, I am."

"What are you doing in Ohio? Are you just visiting here?"

"No, I am here for my job. I work here."

The conversation continued going back and forth about why Hardy Jr. was in the area, where he was headed to, and why he had a California car in town. It never seemed to satisfy the officer as to why Hardy was in Ohio with this car! I heard him ask Hardy Jr. at least eight times why he had a car from California in that region, and also if the car was his car! OK, flashbacks of our other police encounters started to haunt me. Hardy Jr. kept answering the officer's questions, but it apparently was not sufficient. I began to get unnerved from the questions I was hearing the cop continually ask, and I couldn't help myself. I blurted out, "Tell him where you work, Hardy! Why you have your car in Ohio!" (I wanted Hardy to simply tell him that he was a Cincinnati Bengal, which could help explain why his car was from another state. It was common for pro athletes to import their cars seasonally to wherever they played.)

Then I thought about what I had just done. Oh no! I did what he asked me not to do. I was so consumed with the fear of that cop not believing Hardy Jr. I just wanted him to fully understand the circumstances. From the conversation I heard; it did not seem that the officer believed Hardy. Somehow, there was a tone of disbelief and a hint of suspicion in his voice. He had kept asking about the car. His tone and voice inflections (This is YOUR car? This car belongs to YOU?) sounded familiar. His questions seemed as if he was doubtful that the car really was Hardy Jr.'s, which then presented the possibility of further suspicions and probing — just getting deeper and deeper into an

exchange that did not need to evolve in such a way. So much unnecessary questioning, in my opinion. Hmmm. Was the problem that it was a Mercedes? A young black man driving a Mercedes in a rich part of town? I could not be sure, but it sure reminded me of other encounters we had experienced.

One more time, the officer asked if Hardy Jr. was the owner of the car and wanted the reason for him being there (on the street he was taking to get to Cryotherapy.) It was as if he was trying to catch him telling a lie or giving a different story. He referenced the California driver's license he was studying again and told Hardy Jr. that he needed to know how long he had been in Ohio and for what purposes. He also asked insistently, "So do you know someone here? Are you just driving through?"

Again, Hardy stated simply, "I am a California resident, and I shipped my car out here because I work here in Ohio." Dissatisfied with the cop's persistent questioning and the tone that I detected, I again blurted out, "Tell him about the Bengals!!" And that's when my son disconnected the call! He hung up on me! I immediately started to panic! I realized that I had overstepped boundaries by interjecting myself into the conversation, which the officer could hear over the speakers. But I was only trying to help! I was afraid for my son's safety after hearing how the conversation was going.

The officer clearly had an issue of some sort with Hardy Jr., and I was desperately afraid for his life. From what I was hearing, this was not the old "if you don't do anything wrong, then you have nothing to worry about" gig. My mind began to race and think about all of the horrible ways the exchange could get worse, and without Hardy Jr. having a witness! He had just disconnected what I considered my lifeline to him in such a potentially dangerous situation. I immediately called my husband to tell him the story of what had just happened. "Please, please, please try to call Hardy Jr.

Maybe he will answer the phone if it's you!" I was so shaken. I had tried calling Hardy Jr. again and he refused to pick up. At that point I began running back home. I waited to hear what Hardy Sr. might find out, but he was unable to reach him either. Once I got back home (about 7 minutes later), I contacted our friend Q, who we had known for years and who specializes in training law enforcement officers. He actually had written a book specifically geared toward instructing us about how to handle police stops and detailing the do's and don'ts concerning interactions with the police.

Q responded immediately, and we then exchanged messages about the incident. I soon learned that my husband (who had since left to go to work) had finally gotten through to Hardy Jr. and that he was OK. The officer wrote him a ticket for speeding and finally let him go. I was relieved to hear that he was fine, and Hardy Sr. told me he explained to Jr. how worried I was and not to ever hang up on a call during a traffic stop again. Meanwhile, Q called me to see how I was doing and to find out how Hardy Jr. was doing. One other bit of information that was revealed was that my son had refused to tell the officer that he was an NFL player because he had been instructed to do so by the team. (That's a subject for another time, but I wholeheartedly disagreed with that philosophy and felt that revealing his team affiliation just might be the "saving grace" in a tense situation such as that one.) Thankfully, all ended positively in that my son was alive, and there had not been any hostile progression to the encounter. I was relieved, but at the same time, disturbed by it all. I thought about how my family seemed to have so many issues with police (and non-police) over our cars! Whether speeding or not (and many times I was not convinced we had been speeding), attitudes of suspicion and indignation about our cars - or about US driving these cars - seemed to always materialize.

Police always asking us, aggressively and condescendingly, if this is our car. Here's a novel thought – Why wouldn't it be?! Again, I wondered –

Would they have asked a white person, "Is this your car" over eight times? Can we ever experience the paradigm shift where the possibility of black people driving luxury cars, owning expensive items, residing in affluent areas, assuming authority positions of power, and just living their best lives is routinely accepted? Expected? Especially by the police? And if so, should there be any need to register disbelief or shock that this is the reality?

How I reacted to Hardy Jr.'s traffic stop is yet another example of the fear most black people are plagued with. We can be minding our own business and then, just like that, have to shoulder the burden of proof to convince others that we are who we say we are, are where we are supposed to be, are owners of what we say we own. This is all so problematic. What's that they say about Constitutional rights? And all of the fear involved is simply not right. In a nutshell –

WE. ARE. AFRAID.

Just like many white people say they are of us.

- We are afraid that someone will think we look suspicious, and then call the police, and then....

- We are afraid that we will "fit the description."

- We are afraid of what could transpire during a "routine" traffic stop. You see, we have watched hours and hours of footage of our people obeying and complying, and still being fatally shot.

- We are afraid of what you might THINK you see, however outlandish that may be WHEN YOU SEE US.

- And we are most afraid of the reality that our fears do not seem to get the same response as when YOU are afraid. All of this certainly takes a heavy toll.

SIX

THE HEAVY TOLL

I feel that I can confidently speak for the majority of African Americans, or black people, when I say that our lives go interrupted, on a daily basis, navigating the terrain created by racism and a racist society. I cannot think of a day when I am not consciously making decisions to either avert a white person's suspicion or going out of my way to be "OK" for white America. I routinely go through scenes like these:

Let's see – I'm going downtown today – I better not wear sweats, just in case.

I'd like to look for a purse at Saks – Oh, wait, I can't wear this outfit. I better put on makeup, too, and carry my Gucci purse when I go in there. Look the part. Oh, wait. They might think I took the purse. Hmmmmm.

Oh no, son. Please don't wear that hoodie today. You know you're going out to (insert any affluent, upscale area). Take it off. Yes, I know it's cold, but find another jacket. And keep your hands out of your pockets, too. OK, you have a great day. Love you.

Oh no, son. You can't wear that hoodie to the barbershop. You know you're going to (insert any known area of town populated with black people). Lots of cops over there all the time. I don't need them mistaking you for a

criminal. Take it off. Yes, I know it's cold, but find another jacket.

Oh, hey, sweetie! Don't get gas over in (insert any affluent, upscale area) today. You know. Just don't need any trouble.

Oh, yes. I'll go ahead and take this iPhone. That's all I needed to buy. Oh, no, you don't have any more white ones in stock? Oh darn. No, I don't want a black

iPhone. I really came here to get a white one. Yes, I'm sure. No, I don't want a black phone. I am always carrying my phone, especially when I run, and I do not need it to resemble a weapon. Thanks, I'll wait on your next shipment. Please give me a call when the white phones are in stock.

Hello. Oh, yes, hi there. Oh, you're on your way out here? Oh, OK. No, don't follow the GPS directions. I'll tell you how to come. I don't want you going through X part of town. You know, they have been stopping a lot of us over there. So, I want you to take the X freeway and come around through X. Yes, I realize it takes longer, but just to be safe. Come the way I'm telling you, OK?

Hey, Hardy. Let's go for a walk. Come on. Oh, wait. Actually, let me put on my UC Berkeley sweatshirt. You know, just so they know. Yeah, I'm educated. Represent.

The idea that my day-to-day life constitutes a preemptive process of de-escalation – whether involving police officers or just plain, average white people assuming the role of enforcer – is absurd. It is dehumanizing. Time-consuming. Wearisome. It is also, unfortunately, my reality. I must always be prepared. I am always anticipating a "situation." Black people have to work so many angles, daily, just to exist on this planet. Hoping that nothing or no one threatens our right to exist.

We warn our children, repeatedly, to watch out. We buy books helping us identify specific steps geared toward preventing harm, or de-escalating situations with police. We prepare checklists. Scripts. We make preparations for "The Talk." We have "The Talk." We hold discussions after "The Talk." We give daily reminders about "The Talk." We make weekly updates to "The Talk." After we're done with that, then there's "The Look" that we all recognize and must discuss. To the point of exhaustion. And continually playing "what

if" games in your mind whenever you spot a white person, or an officer because ...you just don't know. We just never know. And that's heavy. Boy, is it ever heavy! And despite all of the preparations and rehearsals that we put our kids through, the reality that none of the training will ever completely shield them from being wrongfully accused or harassed presents levels of stress so extreme and toxic that we literally put our lives at risk just anticipating the "what ifs." That heaviness is compounded every single time another negative encounter occurs. It is as if you are continually wrapped in a cocoon of dread and despair, constantly holding your breath, hoping that things don't spiral out of control and threaten your existence.

I am reminded of the time I received a phone call from our oldest daughter, Ashleigh, about another "run-in" with police. Ashleigh is the same poor child who was in the back seat of our car during the terrifying traffic stop near Tallahassee, where she witnessed the Florida state trooper interrogate us with his gun drawn!

As I mentioned in one of the stories I told earlier in the book, she was completely traumatized by the incident. She was only three years old, but that experience was imprinted in her cellular memory, and she has never forgotten how that made her feel. All it takes is a "trigger" and, unfortunately, those stored memories flood the senses. I could tell by the tone of her voice immediately that she had sunken to a new level of weary. Here is what had happened to her that day that became her latest trigger:

One Sunday morning during her Spring semester in 2010, Ashleigh had gone on an outing with about a dozen and a half of her fellow teammates and a few other student-athletes from school. She was in her freshman year at UC Berkeley and was a member of the Women's track team. A bunch of them had helped to plan a friend's birthday celebration at one of the bay area's popular paintball compounds. College student-athletes have extremely rigid schedules, so the only time they would have to plan something like this would

be on a Sunday when they had no classes, practices or training sessions. Ashleigh's group, which was comprised of 18-20-year-olds, took several cars to the outing and enjoyed competing in fun paintball games for a few hours, but then realized as noon was approaching that there was no food available there. Everyone was famished, so they decided to head over to a nearby Pizza Hut. Once they got there, they realized that this particular Pizza Hut did not have dine-in facilities, so they could only order the pizza to carry out. None of the kids in the group thought it was a problem to eat the pizzas in the parking lot since there was nowhere else to go. Once their large order was ready, everyone gathered in the parking lot. Some ate their pizza inside their cars, and others placed their pizza boxes on the hoods of their cars and stood around eating, talking and having a good time.

The next thing Ashleigh knew, a police car rolled up, and a white police officer hopped out of the car and yelled, "Stop! Put the pizza boxes on the ground!"

Ashleigh said everyone was surprised and just did not know what was going on. The officer then proceeded to tell them, "We've gotten a call that there's a fight. I was told that there were 30 people here fighting." The kids all registered shock at the allegation. 30?! How did they come up with such a large number?! One of them spoke up and said, "No one is fighting. It's a birthday!"

The officer again ordered them to put the pizza boxes on the ground, and, at that point, another one of Ashleigh's friends asked, "Why? We're not doing anything." Then some more police cars showed up on the scene, and it was their behavior and aggression that really shocked the kids. Ashleigh said that in no time at all, there were six cop cars at the scene of Pizza Hut where these kids were only trying to eat some pizza and enjoy themselves. Once the backup cars arrived, the officers got out with their hands on "something." Ashleigh explained that it was not clear what their hands were on – they could not tell if it was their guns

or Tasers, but their aggressive behavior and inability to try to talk to them without acting defensive shook them all. Some of the officers that had arrived after the first one were standing outside of their cars and were not fully visible; they positioned themselves behind the open doors, which partially shielded them and whatever was in their hands. This was just too much!

Complete terror! To put this situation in context, this incident was occurring not long after an Oakland BART police officer had shot and killed unarmed BART rider Oscar Grant, a black man, in the early morning hours of New Year's Day. It had been over a year, but the unjust killing had sparked outrage throughout the entire bay area and had caused numerous protests and even some rioting. This predated Trayvon Martin's murder and the host of other killings of unarmed black men and women that have chilled the nation to this day, but suffice it to say, the close proximity to where Oscar Grant lost his life struck a nerve with countless young people. Considering the way in which those officers were acting in the Pizza Hut parking lot, there was no telling what else would happen, in their minds. So, Ashleigh and her friends were all in shock. Oscar Grant was fresh on their minds. It was not unreasonable to think about how all Oscar Grant had intended to do was go celebrate the New Year in San Francisco, yet his life was snuffed away unnecessarily by an overly aggressive cop. He had done nothing wrong but lost his life anyway. Would they meet the same fate?

Ashleigh said these thoughts raced through her mind and she later learned, after the incident, that everyone else was just as scared and thinking the same thoughts. She also remembered the state trooper who had his gun drawn for no reason, and she then felt even worse. The stress in this situation was intense! Ashleigh also noticed the racial dynamics of the situation. All of the police officers that had shown up were white males. And all of the college students were Black, with the exception of two Polynesians. Besides

that fact, who in the world even called the cops and told them that there were 30 people fighting in the parking lot?! Another exaggeration about the numbers present. There certainly were not 30 people there, let alone any of them fighting! Ashleigh was livid, but at the same time, very afraid of what might transpire.

Still watching the police officers in their stances (with their hands on whatever they were holding) as if there was going to be some sort of "action" soon, no one in the group moved. Perhaps it was because actually moving to place a pizza box on the ground could have been misconstrued as a "sudden movement" or maybe one of the officers would "fear for their life" and then shoot. What a horrific predicament to be in! And, for what?! No one was breaking any law. And no one had been given the chance to even explain what was actually going on and why they were there. It was as if there was immediate judgment based on some unknown person's phone call and that was all the cops were going to rely on.

Finally, one of the kids spoke up to the head officer and said, "Sir, it is our friend's birthday. We are all Cal students who are just trying to celebrate his birthday. No one has been fighting. Can you please leave us alone?" Then the officer told them sternly, "You can't be here!" Then Ashleigh's friend asked, "OK, but can we finish eating?" The officer snapped, "Finish eating and then get out of here!" At that point, most of the pizza had already been consumed, so there was little left to finish. And even if there was food left to eat, under the circumstances, they all knew it was time to go. Ashleigh said they all just looked around at one another and sensed that they had to leave, so they began to stack the empty pizza boxes in their cars and prepared to leave the premises, all while the cops were still watching them. Some of the officers got back into their cars, and the rest remained standing in their spots, glaring at the group. Once everyone had gotten into their cars, they slowly drove off and began their trip headed back to Berkeley.

When talking to Ashleigh during our phone call, where she was clearly shaken and outraged, she mentioned how utterly ridiculous she and her friends felt the police officers' actions were. Yet, they were defenseless, and that made it feel even worse. Ashleigh rattled off all of the reasons why this was so senseless to her – "It was just a birthday celebration! It was Sunday at 12:30! In the middle of the day! No one was doing anything wrong! No one was drinking or smoking or anything like that! We didn't even have any music playing! All we were trying to do was eat our food!" And all I could do was offer my support, tell her I understood, and then I became even angrier that this was a reality that seemed like it would never change. Were we not meant to have joy? Would the police have been called if it were a group of white kids eating pizza in the parking lot? Where else are you supposed to eat when there is no dine-in area where you have just spent your money on food? All of these thoughts rushed my mind. What is even more disturbing is that they were never told by the establishment that they could not eat on site. As my mother always said, "You can't win for losing." And the emotional weight of this encounter sucked a little more life out of my child when all she wanted to do was BE. A heavy toll, indeed.

I recently was explaining to a friend of mine how all of this "just sucks away from my soul." I shared how, every day, I wake up hoping that we don't get another "story"...and then, there's another "story!" It feels like I am stuck in an endless loop - repeating, repeating, repeating- messages that I will never feel safe. The pain and fright that all of these encounters, or fear of potential encounters, creates robs us of our lives. It's not simply enough to not get shot, or not have the police called on you, or not get into an altercation with someone who views you as the "other." When our very skin elicits responses from whites, no matter what we are doing, or not doing, it becomes burdensome navigating the possible outcomes of everything. The feeling of dread and despair caused by the reality that you are only one accusation away from death is heavy.

This feeling is something that cannot just go away. It remains. For many of us, our presence at this time in such a polarized, dangerous world creates trauma and even PTSD. It literally makes us sick. And then, the thing is that all of these preventive, preemptive attempts to avoid instantaneous judgments of suspicion or guilt sometimes work and sometimes don't. We still go through the motions, though, just in case. But, damn, it sure does take a lot of effort. And, for the most part, white people don't have to do this. Don't have to have a non-stop thought machine running, computing all of the "what ifs" and possible scenarios that could go down if X, Y, or Z happens.

That is what we mean when we refer to "white privilege." Compared to black people, whites enjoy the privilege and FREEDOM of not having to go through all of these hoops that I am describing, in most instances. They have the privilege of just BEING, without any necessary adjustments to allow for external factors that could threaten their acts of being or even their very lives. Black people don't normally get to do that. We must resort to living extremely calculated lives, depending on the minutiae of every situation. There is no other way to put it other than to say it is all just plain exhausting. And, despite what many people think about the lives of professional athletes and celebrities, being a black one is really overrated. Because, despite all of the hard work that goes into achieving the fame and fortune, there is still nothing to protect you from a racist society ready to suspect or to react negatively. Ready to say they are afraid. Ready to call cops. Ready to kill you first and ask questions later.

The stress of having to exist under such conditions is enormous. And there has been quite a bit of research conducted to quantify the damage from such stress and traumatic events, particularly concerning mental health. One such study, conducted by researchers in collaboration from the University of Pennsylvania, Boston University, and Harvard, concludes that police

killings "have harmed mental health in black communities" (Eligon, 2018). Their study was intended to be "a significant attempt to assess the measurable, if indirect, harms that police violence has inflicted on the broader psychological and emotional well-being of African-Americans." The lead researcher, Dr. Atheendar S. Venkataramani, has described the stressful effects on African-Americans as "observable and real" and also suggests the impact runs even deeper, as their findings are just "the tip of the iceberg."

So, we are not exaggerating after all! What so many of us say that we feel time after time after time is supported by empirical research. Of course, this single study measured the negative effects related to police violence specifically, but there is still even more stress from racism, in general. In addition to all of the other physical health crises that we face within our communities – diabetes, obesity, high blood pressure, cancer, to name a few - it is unacceptable that we must also battle deteriorating mental health as a result of how we are perceived, and ultimately policed. This is quite a heavy toll just to try to exist in America. For all of us, even the "rich and famous." Still, many high-profile athletes and entertainers or people of means have some ways of diverting or remedying some trouble. At least we can live in neighborhoods that are relatively safe (even if neighbors don't always recognize us as belonging there.) We can afford lawyers; we often have access to resources many others may not have access to, and sometimes can summon help from other people in "high places."

Of course, this means nothing if we are dead. And that is a real possibility in a "trigger happy" country where everyone wants to try to stand their ground, and even stand your ground while claiming it's their ground. I should not be witnessing the very things my mother and father (who were born and raised in the Jim Crow South) told me about. The very same things they lived through in the 40's, 50's, 60's....oh yeah, and the 70's, 80's, 90's, the new millennium. How far have we

come again?! Many of us obey the laws. We toe the line. We do what we shouldn't even have to do most times to try to prove we are not threats. But still, something invariably goes down because we seem threatening. Dangerous. Suspicious. Whatever. We have witnessed numerous white people's credibility go unquestioned when they express their "fears" or "suspicions." We also have seen many white cops say, "I feared for my life," regardless of the circumstances, and their versions of what transpired are usually believed. Where do we go from here? It often boils down to our word against theirs. Even with video footage proving otherwise, we have often had to bear the weighty burdens of injustice.

The serious issue of black people being perceived and viewed as threats must stop, or nothing else really matters. Body cameras, being polite, keeping hands visible, and not wearing hoodies. Whatever all the hoops are that we must go through (that whites usually aren't expected to) do not matter if white people continue to make unjustified claims of suspicion and guilt, and act on those hunches. Being a good person may still not be enough. Being a model citizen may not be enough. I wonder what it would feel like to never have to carry this burden? For my body, my mind, my nervous system, my heart not to have to take such a massive hit? My final seven words to sum up all of this:

WHAT. ELSE. DO. WE. HAVE. TO. DO?!

SEVEN

A SENSE OF HUMANITY, PLEASE

"Can we all get along?" – Rodney King

First, the Rodney King beating of 1991. Then, the Rodney King-related riots of 1992. What are we witnessing nearly thirty years later? Will we ever be able to get along? Not to delve into the King case too extensively, but suffice it to say, the jury's decision to acquit the four white police officers responsible for beating Rodney King to a pulp led to the infamous LA riots of 1992 (which some say was one of the worst moments of racial unrest in American history.)

Those riots, which lasted for six days, caused 55 deaths, over 2,000 injuries, and led to the arrest of over 11,000 people (Walker, 2017)! If you aren't familiar with this historic event, the root of it all was the unjustified, excessive violence unleashed on King and the blatant disregard for a just verdict via the criminal justice system. We had witnessed Rodney King's savage beating at the hands of merciless white cops. They repeatedly kicked him and beat him with a baton (30+ hits) for a reported 15 minutes. There was no question about the brutality. At that point, every black person that I knew was, first, flabbergasted and then outraged. We had SEEN the video of the unjustified violence. Millions of TV viewers had seen the video, shown over and over and over again. That was the first time America had a chance to see police officers brutalize someone who posed no threat at all, so atrociously on camera. And, without question, most of us just KNEW that the footage of the beating would count for something.

For the defense, Rodney King's rights had clearly been violated. Certainly, for a jury to know, without a doubt, that Rodney King had not posed a threat to the

officers and that use of excessive force was completely unnecessary. And, yet, the justification was that Rodney King did pose a threat after all. He supposedly "charged" one of the officers, according to the police report, but this was not found to be true based on the video footage that we all saw. Even if Rodney King had posed a threat, it certainly did not justify the beating that seemed to last forever.

This, undeniably, was another case of a black man who instilled fear in the minds of the responding officers, and "how they saw him" supposedly made them feel justified in doing what they did. Their minds somehow processed the belief that King lunged at and charged them. Consequently, those guilty cops were found NOT guilty! Even with all of the captured footage showing King NOT presenting a threat. The message was loud and clear. Apparently, seeing was actually NOT believing. And that is what spun black America out of control in 1992, and prompted Rodney King, the victim at the root of it all, to make his famous plea for an end to the violence during a televised news conference. CAN WE ALL GET ALONG? Here we are, in 2019, grappling with the same problems. How is it that not much has changed in almost 30 years?! Even scarier, hypothetically, if we wait around 30 more years under these same conditions, how many more could wind up victims of police brutality? Or worse, unjustly incarcerated? Or dead? What will "the stories" be like in 2049?

We now live in a society where everyone is equipped to be a photojournalist and can capture every word, every move. However, viral cell phone footage, like the footage of Rodney King's beating, has not changed the fact that there are still some police officers out there who behave unethically (like planting a Taser or a gun near the victim's body in order to frame a specific narrative about what actually happened.)

All too often, we see police officers (and as I have discussed, non-police as well) justifying unnecessary

actions against black and brown people. And as cell phone footage also shows us, they are less likely to use excessive force against, or to kill, whites. We know that police officers are highly skilled and are trained to de-escalate and deal with many dangerous situations; we watch them do it effectively with white people all the time. So, in comparison, why is it so difficult for black people to be treated in the same way?

Clearly, we know what we see. And, frankly, a disturbing number of them don't seem to care that we do see. As I have already explained, this is what creates more angst, more panic, more fear, more anger. The notion that you can have proof of something so horrific, and it can just get dismissed, is outrageous — no sense of justice. The Rodney King beating (and more current ones caught on camera, like Eric Garner gasping while exclaiming "I Can't Breathe" until he took his last breath, and unarmed Stephon Clark being gunned down while holding an iPhone in his hand) have represented a wakeup call for us. The realization that even what we

COULD prove with video footage was still not enough to support our claims of abuse and misconduct. We had no way of being protected because, even if we recorded an incident, it still might not matter.

Seeing was believing, but somehow, the conclusions based on the visual evidence were explained away, or they were simply ignored. Somehow designations of "threat" and accusations of aggression, causing cops to "fear for their lives," became the norm. Or continued to be the norm even when it was clear that this was not the truth. Rodney King's abusers, after fracturing his skull and causing permanent brain damage, breaking bones in his face and ankle, knocking out teeth, and causing numerous lacerations, were not held accountable for their actions. And anyone who saw the footage should have concluded that King was treated worse than an animal. Just the visuals of Rodney King during and after the beating, alone, are enough to create fear within a community. Yet, today, we are inundated with so many

more visuals. Routine visuals. SO routine that we often just check Twitter or social media news feeds, searching to find out whether or not there is another "story."

As for that rhetorical question posed by Rodney King - CAN we get along? I believe that, in King's case and countless other cases of black men, women, and children being violently beaten or killed, something happens well before any heated exchange or altercation or attempt to arrest occurs. It goes much deeper – it goes back to what I have said happens "when they see us." Just like the Central Park 5 were portrayed as animals, even though they had not committed the crimes they were accused of, we have a huge problem in America with the inability to value the lives of black people.

As I have detailed throughout this book, something gets triggered in some people when they see us, and the interpretation of who we are does not allow any possibility for equality. Or a sense of humanity. Everything basically revolves around how we are seen, and what feelings are aroused once we are seen, assessed, and judged. "When they see us," do we even stand a chance? What is the solution? The truth is, although most law officers do the right thing and try to abide by the law, we are not merely dealing with "a few bad apples."

Based on what we continue to see play out across the country, it is clear that the problems stemming from bad policing (and vigilante civilians behaving badly) are institutional and systemic in nature. These horrible displays of injustice and inhumanity that continue to haunt us are symptomatic of a larger problem – (cough) America's problem with race. And truthfully, it is our entire society that must change, not just police officers. America knows it has a problem, but, corporately, we can never seem to adequately address it head-on. Many people prefer to skirt around the issue. Remain in denial. Blame the victim. Not call a spade a spade. And

then, consequently, bad things continue to happen. We have eruption after eruption because we have never adequately dealt with it. And, for the most part, it is white people (not all, of course) who choose to remain in denial about how poorly black and brown people are still treated today, even when we can plainly see that it is a fact.

We can openly see instances of blatant injustice today, and after reviewing the "tape," how we were treated last year, and in 2016, 2015, 2014, 2008, 2005, 1995, 1992, 1989, 1974, the 1960's, and as far back as we are able to access documentation of the atrocities. These are problems that must be urgently discussed. How we even got here in the first place, under what conditions, and how our disenfranchisement within American society is still up for debate! In fact, many schools still choose not to present entire factual accounts of our difficult past, particularly concerning slavery. It is America's dirty secret that is often pushed back deep into the closet because, if it is not visible, then surely it must not exist. But racist sentiments and actions continue. Oppression continues. The failure to successfully engage in productive dialogue about past wrongs, systemic racist practices, and how the victims of such treatment actually FEEL is a major problem.

Like other societal problems, such as alcoholism or compulsive gambling, those acting out their problems many times do not want to come to grips with the roots of the problem. Many of them deny that they have a problem, even when it is clearly evident that they do. I had an uncle who was an alcoholic and who denied his entire life that he was one. He would frequent neighborhood liquor stores and would drink any and every type of alcohol he could find (as my mother would say, jokingly – even acid, shoe polish, or lye) – it didn't matter what it was; he just had to have alcohol. Even after having passed out in the street, he would deny he was an alcoholic. He was incapable of admitting that truth. He refused to acknowledge reality. So, it is with racism.

This is why we keep seeing such heated arguments about the subject. Turn on one channel, and you will see black people, fed up with the denials, outlining incident after incident (as I have done in this book) as proof that we live in a racist nation. They call for white people to face it, admit it, and stop perpetuating it. Turn on a different channel, and you will see apologists denying it, vilifying the victims of it, and sometimes even lashing out challenging those who don't like it to get out of the country, where they presumably don't belong, at least in their minds!

People who are racists believe they are superior to other groups. They believe that "others" have caused or could cause the demise of their neighborhoods, their cities, their schools, their beloved nation. They believe that "others" have certain tendencies and characteristics, such as crime, delinquency, dishonesty, ignorance, low intellect, immorality, laziness, filth, and squalor.

When entire systems have been designed and built by these types of people and, consequently, their racist ideologies and practices are woven into the fabric of those systems, then it is no wonder that an entire nation can be infected with the "virus." The educational system. Banking system. Healthcare industry. Insurance industry. Entertainment industry. Media. Criminal justice system. Transportation. Housing. Religion. Just about everything has been affected and influenced by institutionalized racism and structural inequities in America. We all must acknowledge this. Furthermore, we must do all we can to have the conversations – those hard conversations – about how people feel about race and racism. And what can be done to eliminate it.

When black people (and other minority groups) tell their stories about horrific treatment and why they believe it to be race-related, there is the tendency for some to accuse us of playing "the race card." That has to stop. Please believe us. Empathize with us. Bad things really have happened and continue to happen.

And, as I have shared many times, often because of our race. If this is not addressed, and if people are not believed and their stories simply dismissed as attempts to "race bait," then it will be to our peril. We have to be able to talk about past wrongs and the pain that people feel as a result of the wrongdoing that is still being perpetuated. And about how deeply racism in America has damaged and destroyed people and their communities. Whether that is talking about slavery, segregation, unfair hiring practices, redlining, immigration, white supremacist groups, police killings, profiling, whatever, the approach to finding a solution is the same.

We must first acknowledge, then apologize for wrongdoings, and then ultimately work towards solutions. For different outcomes. For reconciliation and the ability to co-exist peacefully. But, to reiterate, we must first believe that there has been wrongdoing. The wrongs can no longer be ignored, explained away, rationalized, justified, or just figuratively swept into a corner with the hope that, over time, they will disappear. Because, of course, they never just disappear. Instead, they fester, increasing in toxicity as time goes on. There is no expiration date on the offenses that have yet to be healed, even if those offenses occurred 50 years ago, or 100 years, or 200, or more. Nearly thirty years ago, I simply had no idea that thirty years in the future, we would be having the same exact problems that I had witnessed and experienced as a college student, and to some degree, even worse than anything I had ever seen in my lifetime. I had hoped for and expected constant progress in our society, in our world. Yet, avoiding the tough conversations and remaining in denial stymies any true progress at all.

In thinking about what needs to happen to improve our relations with law enforcement, it is critical that we begin to have those conversations. We must air out our grievances and discuss the reasons why we have so much fear of the police, why tensions are so high, and why so many of them seem to fear us. Why many in the

community are reactive and defensive. When you continue to deal with racist encounters, as my family has countless times, your "stories" must be told and hopefully believed. And then there is the issue of trust. One reason why we can't seem to "get along" is because of the lack of trust. Referencing an insightful quote, I saw posted on social media (author unknown), "There are two reasons why we don't trust people. First – we don't know them. Second – we know them." Concerning black people who fear police and do not trust them, both of these reasons do apply.

Countless communities still have not been fully embraced by law enforcement to be able to become "comfortable" with their presence. Many simply do not feel that they know them well enough to trust them. Although there are many instances where we see police officers making it a point to engage with communities of color, it does not happen nearly enough. To really get to know the people they serve will ultimately encourage police officers to consider their humanity at all times. The same is true about all of the non-police folks trying to police black and brown lives. Most of us in the black community desire positive relationships with law enforcement because we want our families and property to be safe, too. We want relationships with officers who know us and respect us. Who interact with us and treat us like human beings, not animals. Many of the issues that plague our relationships with law enforcement can be alleviated or eliminated by making strides toward knowing and understanding the community better.

Conversely, the second part of the quote about trust – not trusting people because you DO know them – is the bigger issue. A lack of trust remains because we DO see what keeps happening. We do see what they do. And we can see what they believe through their actions. We have seen too many deaths at the hands of police officers, officers who seemed not to value the lives of black and brown people. We have watched, ad nauseam, innocent black and brown people get shot in

the head, in the chest, or in the back while running away, completely unarmed. We have watched them get punched, kicked, Tased or sprayed with Mace until their skin is on fire. We have watched grandmothers get manhandled and slammed to the ground. Pregnant women and young girls, too.

Many of us feel that we are walking black and brown targets; our skin always being perceived as dangerous. Maya Angelou's famous quote – "When people show you who they are, believe them" also seems to apply here. Our personal stories about how we have been treated by police officers create the narrative from which we come to "know" them or know about them. Thus, many of us believe that, based on what we have seen and keep seeing, "we know you." And that knowing is generally not positive. Worse, it serves to corroborate all of the generational "stories" that we were told as cautionary tales. We continue to get reminders that give the black community pause about trusting anyone at all.

Yet, we must ultimately figure out a way to trust, and the trust must go BOTH WAYS. In order to achieve this, there must be institutional changes whereby the value of black lives and the potential that exists within every black body, along with the potential of all other members of the human race, is seriously considered. Everyone must be educated so that they understand what has occurred to create the crises that we continue to see today, and ultimately gain the awareness that ALL people's lives are gifts that are worthy of protection and preservation. Additionally, in order for police officers to be trusted within the black community or any community for that matter, there must be signs or proof that true justice is achievable. That blind justice is even possible.

As of now, every time we see negative outcomes involving law enforcement, especially unjustified deaths as a result of questionable practices or impulsive decisions, all efforts to promote trust and improved relations take another hit. So that is why it is

imperative for law enforcement agencies to prioritize making the communities they serve feel less marginalized. There needs to be an all-out effort to convince us that we can trust them. Going back to what I stated earlier regarding racism in America, the level of trust can change for the better once racism is acknowledged and condemned. We all have to come to grips with the fact that the criminal justice system and law enforcement agencies, like all other systems, have been tainted and corrupted, and there is a pervasive culture of racial bias within these systems that must be weeded out.

Racism and racist practices are undeniably baked into the culture. And the thing is, some within the system fail to realize that they are even racists or behave differently when engaging with minorities. If you ask a person if they are racist, they will invariably answer "NO." Many don't believe they are. Yet they continue to exhibit behaviors consistent with racism or bigotry. Similarly, racist police officers will rarely, if ever, acknowledge that they are racists and that they "see" black people differently than whites. But there are many studies proving that this does occur. Considering the frightening stories, I have shared in this book, I would venture to say that many of those who acted out unnecessarily probably were racists, or at the very least held biased views about who they thought we were or what we might do, based on stereotypes of black people. People with those tendencies need to be rooted out or properly trained and educated to understand why their beliefs are not in alignment with a diverse and inclusive world. So, what must we do? How can we ensure that "when they see us," it is not through lenses tainted with racial bias, prejudice, and disdain? How do we begin to make positive strides so that we can "all get along?"

Obviously, finding ways to implement effective training guidelines and proper training to improve policing practices is of paramount concern. The selection process for new officers is also a huge

concern. One of the biggest needs is to be able to develop more policies and offer officers more training in the prevention of racial profiling. Law enforcement agencies must guard against racism and prejudice before it ever hits the streets. This can be accomplished first through the selection process. Those under consideration for positions in law enforcement must be able to demonstrate that they espouse values consistent with the agency's goals of fairness, diversity, and inclusion.

Any history of racial bias must be addressed, possibly corrected through training. Yet, even with the best-designed programs, it can still be difficult to identify and adequately measure indicators of implicit bias and prejudice.

Some officers may have deeply-engrained biases that are not detected with routine implicit bias testing and training, and subtle racist ideologies, which can lead to ill-conceived notions of threat or suspicion, might be hard to detect. Police officers should also continually be tested or undergo interviews to help detect any traits consistent with poor judgment abilities. Same with screening regarding personality types – ideal officers should not be highly reactive or short-tempered. Not that that alone will fix all the problems, but it seems that many of the officers who have committed acts of violence and brutality against minorities acted extremely aggressively. Perhaps this could be identified before having such a person out on the streets? Is some sort of psychological assessment measuring potential racial animosity out of the question?

Having no real experience with the administration side of law enforcement, I am simply making suggestions that seem viable to me, but I am really not sure about the extent to which officers can be subjected to such testing. It just seems like a good idea and a possible way to help deal with these pervasive issues. I also do not find unreasonable to implement the

necessary training around issues of suspicion and race. Profiling falls into this category as well, but police officers must be educated on the fears that innocent people have or develop as a result of their acts of suspicion.

Unjustified suspicion of black and brown people can lead to unwarranted harassment, or arrests, or even death, as we all have seen. Along those lines, law enforcement agencies must somehow devise ways to deconstruct the whole "fear of blackness" phenomenon. It is difficult to predict how some police officers will behave during those split-second moments where they often come to believe they must fear for their lives when, in reality, no real threat exists. Many times, this is race-related, and supposed fears arise, prompting them to behave in manners that are aggressive and provocative. Short of resorting to futuristic measures and pre-crime detection, like we have seen in Sci-Fi movies such as "Minority Report" or similar, there must be a way to gauge an officer's predisposition to certain behaviors. (Yes, I did just mention Minority Report – we need some comic relief at this point.) In all seriousness, some type of research or more effective training must be introduced to eliminate these instantaneous reactions that seem to be "triggered" by black and brown people.

Additionally, law enforcement agencies must take seriously the rampant acts of calling police on black and brown people due to unjustified suspicions. Although not actually police training-related, it is the police that are drawn into investigating these calls to 911, so there needs to be a way to help discourage these unfair practices. In fact, more policies must be created and implemented regarding erroneous reports of suspected crimes and suspicious activity. There must be serious consequences for putting our lives at risk based off of impulsive and unfounded claims of criminality and threat. Our unofficial list of #hashtags continues to grow out of control because of unwarranted suspicions and accusations. These police calls are not just a

nuisance but can have serious implications for the innocent people who are suspected of being criminals. It must stop!

Remember, George Zimmerman was suspicious of Trayvon Martin, and all he did was walk to a store to get candy and a soft drink. Zimmerman called the police, too, but as we all know, that wasn't the end of the story. There must be harsher penalties for those who act as if they can police others when they have no business doing so. They should be prosecuted and subject to fines for indiscriminately creating fear and causing harm for us based on their paranoia of "others." Once they begin to suffer consequences for their racist behavior, which usually involves the use of police manpower, then we might see a reduction in these types of incidents as well.

Another area that police officers must concentrate more on in an effort to help make the communities they serve feel less marginalized, and to rebuild trust, is with community involvement. Rather than assume what might be best for certain communities and indiscriminately assign a host of "best practices" that may or may not support the community, more needs to be done to incorporate feedback and suggestions from the communities that are policed. They can shed light on current policing efforts and share their perspectives on issues that could become problematic for the department. For instance, I have read numerous articles about communities of color that are dissatisfied with various aspects of their local police forces. One issue that has been stressed repeatedly is the appearance of officers being "above the law." A common complaint concerning recent waves of brutality and deaths of black people at the hands of white police officers is that, many times, the officers go unpunished; they are rarely convicted or even prosecuted for their involvement.

Members of these communities that have experienced such traumatic events simply want

accountability. They want to know that their lives are valued and, should an incident occur that involves misconduct, that police officers will also be subject to the law. There is a growing sentiment among black communities that rarely will justice be served when it concerns law enforcement.

There also seems to be growing doubt about some officers' lack of truthfulness and even signs of corruption that could be problematic. Concerned citizens where shooting deaths have taken place claim that many times, video footage that has been captured contradicts the incident reports that police have filed.

Obviously, this is a glaring issue law enforcement agency must address. They must see to it that truth and justice are upheld in these situations, or else the appearances of dishonesty and attempts to cover the truth could ruin community relations and further erode trust. The need for transparency is at an all-time high.

One last thing about police training, accountability, and community involvement. What is even more critical than the introduction and implementation of updated training guidelines or new tools and protocols is the need for them to be effective. Because we have witnessed numerous well-intentioned plans and measures that ultimately fail. For instance, following the wave of police violence against black people that has steadily increased over the past five years, we learned that some police departments had begun requiring the use of body cameras. This was in hopes of being more transparent and creating a way to see every interaction.

That was certainly a step in the right direction. Yet, we still continued to see incidents where police officers were aggressive and used excessive force in their encounters with black people WHILE WEARING THE BODY CAMS! The only difference was that there was now a video record of it, but simply wearing the body cameras did not necessarily change officer

behavior in many cases. It did little to change "how they see us." Even worse, in some instances, police officers have resorted to turning their cameras off, providing no recording at all! When it is time for a review of footage to see exactly what transpired during the altercations or shootings, some have left no trails to study. Consequently, community members are outraged when this occurs because it appears to be deliberate. Thus, it serves little purpose to introduce tools such as body cameras and dashboard cameras, intended to help discourage police misconduct, only to find officers shutting them down. This borders on corruption. The optics of this practice are extremely negative, and it further harms relations between the community and law enforcement. Lack of trust again becomes the main focus.

As much as I have criticized various aspects of law enforcement, and rightly so, I still have a glass-half-full mentality. I believe there is still hope that things can change for the better. Actually, they simply must change. They will not change on their own, though. It will take a concerted effort on many fronts. Still, I believe with a lot of work and commitment to truth, transparency, and fairness, law enforcement in America can experience a positive change in culture. We can even experience reconciliation under the right conditions. What is reconciliation? In my mind, reconciliation essentially means to work out differences in order to move forward.

Acknowledging wrongdoing and making strides to do what Rodney King asked of us. It requires, in my opinion, a level of trust to at least believe that the other "side" or party will work with you to that end. It requires the willingness on the part of those who have caused harm to apologize, to really do better, and not just claim to do better.

It requires putting some of your old beliefs or patterns of behavior to rest, in the interest of reaching a compromise or "happy medium." Lord knows, we

desperately need to experience reconciliation in America, on a number of fronts. But, again, before we can even get to that stage, we first must be able to listen to one another. Really, really listen and then care about what it is that we hear. There also needs to be a sense of urgency regarding instituting restorative measures to make up for the wrongdoing, or to at least express remorse and accept responsibility.

For those of us who have experienced or witnessed mistreatment from police officers, very real fears, and negative memories and scars remain. Yet, we can take our memories and details of the injustices and demand change. It will be people like us who can educate and inform about these injustices, tell our stories so that the world knows what has happened, and what needs to be changed. And then, those actions help to usher in change. Truth and honesty, combined with the willingness to have the necessary conversations we all must have, will be the catalyst for reconciliation. Writing all of these accounts (and, believe it or not, there are still many more left untold) ignited a passion within me to do what I can to bring about social justice and change. I have reflected on all of these issues and occurrences, and, in doing so, things became even more evident. We can no longer afford to continue spiraling to new lows. We all must find a way to get along. I am committed to help bring an end to these horrible practices, beliefs, and attitudes. It is a huge task, and it really can be done, but not....

Until we find a way to decriminalize black and brown people in the minds of everyone;

Until black and brown people can occupy spaces, any space at all, and not elicit cries from whites that they are invading, intruding, unlawfully there;

Until we are stopped during a routine traffic stop and not be terrified of the possibility that it could end in death;

Until my husband, son, or daughters can get into our vehicles without a neighbor calling the police because it looks suspicious;

Until my husband or son can drive down a street in a predominantly white area and not be considered a thief, drug dealer, or person of ill repute;

Until police officers no longer question the legitimacy of our claims that the car belongs to us;

Until I can buy whatever color iPhone I want because I no longer need to prepare ahead of time for potential tragic events;

Until we all are truly innocent until proven guilty.

Finally, we must all rewrite the scripts for what happens "when they see us." The stories really must change. The narrative has to change. In order for any true change to take place, first, THEY must see themselves WHEN THEY SEE US. Once that occurs, there won't be a need to continue with any frames of reference such as "when they see us" or "when we see them" any longer.

Then, we will truly see change.
And, ultimately, we will simply see one another.
And, by then, we just might stand a chance.

HOW DO YOU SEE US?

ACKNOWLEDGMENTS

I want to thank my precious family – my husband, Hardy, my daughters Ashleigh and Haleigh, and my son, Hardy Jr., for your belief in me and my ability to write this book. How I wish that we did not have these disturbing stories to share, but at the very least, I hope that they will open many eyes and lead to positive changes in how we are SEEN and, ultimately, treated. Thanks also, family, for your incredible support, unconditional love and encouragement always. I appreciate you and love you all so very much!

I would also like to thank M. Quentin Williams – better known as Q- for his unwavering excitement and encouragement, and for serving as the catalyst for these stories to be written. You constantly say that "people must tell their stories," and you are the reason this book exists. Your passion for justice and societal reconciliation is contagious, and I am so grateful for your friendship. Thank you for all you have done and continue to do.

Thanks also to my sister from another mother, Dorrie A. Wilson, and my sister-in-law Regina Mason, for all of the support and critical feedback you offered along the way.

The design of the brilliant book cover would not have been possible without the artistic talent and creativity of illustrator Kprecia Ambers and graphic designer Terrence Moline. Thank you so much for capturing the essence of how we are often seen through dark lenses. I also am extremely grateful to Dr. Brenda Combs and BRC Publishing for assisting with the editorial services and publication of this book. I am so very thankful for everyone on my team.

Lastly, thank you to Ava DuVernay for creating her Netflix miniseries *When They See Us,* which spoke to my spirit and helped to provide the framework for expressing my own convictions and outrage about systems, attitudes, and psychological processes that simply must change in my lifetime.

REFERENCES

Alexander, K. (2016). "Who is this Robert Smith? ": A quiet billionaire makes some noise with $20 million gift to the African American museum. In <u>The Washington Post.</u> September 24, 2016. Retrieved from https://www.washingtonpost.com/national/who-is-this-robert-smith-a-quiet-billionaire-makes-some-noise-with-20-million-gift-to-the-african-american-museum/2016/09/23/547da3a8-6fd0-11e6-8365-b19e428a975e_story.html?utm_term=.866987597a20

Downs, K. (2016). FBI warned of white supremacists in law enforcement 10 years ago. Has anything changed? On <u>PBS NewsHour Online</u>. October 21, 2016. Retrieved from https://www.pbs.org/newshour/nation/fbi-white-supremacists-in-law-enforcement

DuVernay, A. (Producer and Director). (2019). *When They See Us.* Forward Movement, Harpo Films, Participant Media & Tribeca Productions. *Netflix.*

Eligon, J. (2018). Police Killings Have Harmed Mental Health in Black Communities, Study Finds. In <u>The New York Times</u>. June 21, 2018. Retrieved from https://www.nytimes.com/2018/06/21/us/police-shootings-black-mental-health.html

Schilling, D. (2015). "When the Color of your Skin is seen as a Weapon, You will Never be seen as Unarmed". On <u>Twitter.</u> August 8, 2015. @DelSchilling. Retrieved from https://twitter.com/DelSchilling/status/630002746872209408

Walker, T. (2017). LA Riots 25 Years Later: Rodney King's "Can we all get along" still matters. In <u>Orange County Register</u>. April 30, 2017. Retrieved from https://www.ocregister.com/2017/04/30/la-riots-25-years-later-rodney-kings-can-we-all-get-along-still-matters/

Williams, M.Q. (2015). A Survival Guide: How NOT To Get KILLED By The POLICE, PART I. Charlotte, NC: Dedication To Community Organization.

Willingham, A.J. (2019). Researchers Studied Nearly 100 Million Traffic Stops And Found Black Motorists Are More Likely To Be Pulled Over. On <u>CNN Online</u>. March 21, 2019. Retrieved from https://www.cnn.com/2019/03/21/us/police-stops-race-stanford-study-trnd/index.html

Amy Nickerson, M.A.

ABOUT THE AUTHOR

Amy Nickerson is a writer, television and film content creator, lecturer, student-athlete educational consultant, and diversity/inclusion/anti-racism advocate. She has counseled countless student-athletes and their families about various issues unique to

student-athletes, such as balancing the demands of school and sports, the NCAA college recruitment process, and general academic support concerns. She has also lectured as a college adjunct instructor focusing on issues concerning black athletes and the educational system.

Amy graduated with honors from the University of California at Berkeley with a Bachelor of Arts degree in Afro-American Studies and Social Sciences. She returned, after a 21-year hiatus spent supporting her husband's pro football career and being "the glue" for her family, to earn a Master of Arts degree in Education from UC Berkeley's Graduate School of Education.

Within the educational community, Amy served for seven years on the Cal Parents Board, the UC Berkeley Library Advisory Board, California Heritage Fund Board, and the Cal Parents' Equity & Inclusion Committee. She has also contributed as a member of numerous other boards and committees focusing on diversity and inclusion, anti-racism, educational equity, and the advancement of multicultural education.

Amy has been married 30 years to husband Hardy, a former NFL All-Pro linebacker and former NFL and college coach. She and her husband are also the parents of three successful young adults, – Ashleigh (recent graduate of UC Hastings College of the Law and Intellectual Property attorney,) Haleigh (recent MFA graduate of Parsons School of Design and multi-media artist/film producer,) and Hardy Jr. (graduate of UC Berkeley - B.A., University of Illinois - M.S., and linebacker for the Cincinnati Bengals.)

Amy and her husband reside in Oakland, CA.

Made in the USA
Lexington, KY
25 November 2019

57681184R00100